Guided Meditation for Chakra Alignment

Activate Chakra Balancing, Cleansing, Healing, and Alignment with Guided Meditation Activation with Positive Energy and Visualization

By Deep Meditation Academy, Timothy Willink

Table of Contents

Introduction

The chakra system has been around since 1500 BC, where it originated in India and was written about in the Vedas. The Vedas were part of some of the earliest Sanskrit literary records. There are seven chakras, each with their own purpose.

They work with different organs and influence your life and body in different ways. The chakras work with your prana, or energy, and they are what keep us vibrant and healthy.

When stimulated, the chakras move from your spine by the tailbone, up to the crown of your head. They can often become blocked, and they can cause various problems. The following are some symptoms of blocked chakras.

If the root chakra is blocked, you may experience anxiety, lower back pain, or issues with your bladder and colon.

A blocked sacral chakra can leave you feeling uninspired, depressed, and with sexual dysfunction.

A blocked solar plexus chakra can create low self-esteem, tummy aches, or problems with procrastination.

A blocked heart chakra can create anger, hatred, and jealousy.

A blocked throat chakra can cause neck stiffness, sore throat ,and affect your ability to speak your truth.

A blocked third-eye chakra can affect your ability to recall facts, cause you to be dismissive, and make you feel dizzy.

A blocked crown chakra can leave you feeling isolated from the world and your spirituality.

Luckily, meditation is a great way to clear out blocked chakras and get them working the way that they should. There are also other practices that you can use along with the meditations to make sure that your chakras remain open and working properly.

These include yoga, eating a balanced diet full of colorful fruits and veggies, aromatherapy, and crystals.

Thank you,

Timothy Willink

How to Get the Most Out of this Book

Meditation should be used every single day to get the most out of it. The meditations are organized into the different chakras and are in order, starting from the base where the root chakra is, and ending with the crown chakra on your head.

Now, you can choose to work a single chakra each day of the week, or you can work on every chakra in one sitting.

When you are starting to work on opening your chakras, it may be best if you do just one chakra a day. You don't want to overwhelm your body or mind, because opening a chakra can create unusual symptoms if you go too quickly.

Before you start a meditation session, make sure you are fully prepared. You need to have enough uninterrupted time to finish the meditation.

Make sure you are fully comfortable and in an article of clothing that won't distract you. This means you should not wear anything tight, noisy, or restrictive. You want to be in loose clothing that you can easily breathe in.

These are best done in a seated, upright position on either a chair or a cushion on the floor. Once you are ready, take a few cleansing breaths to set your mind, and begin.

Root

Color Breathing for the Root Chakra

Get into a comfortable position. If you choose to lie down, allow your entire body to relax and become as comfortable as possible. If you are sitting, let your arms rest. Lay your hands on your lap or the floor. Choose whatever feels the most comfortable for you.

Allow your eyes to float close. This is the time that you have set aside for yourself. Leave all of your worries behind. Let yourself ease into the flow of this meditation. Whatever comes the easiest to you is what is right for you. The only thing that exists is where you are right now. The future and the past are non-existent at this moment.

Take notice of the sounds that are happening outside the room. Acknowledge them and allow them to float away. Take note of any sounds in the room where you are settled. Again, acknowledge them, and allow them to float away.

Let your body know it is time to relax. Allow your legs and feet soften and relax where they are. Let your shoulders fall down your sides. Release any tension you have in your hands. Let your entire body to relax and soften into a natural position.

Have your face and head relax. Feel your hair and scalp soften. Your forehead, eyebrows, eyes, nose, cheeks, chin, jaw, and ears are all softening and relaxing down.

Breathe in a soft and cleansing breath, and exhale all of the tension that you are holding in your body.

Continue to breathe to your own natural rhythm. There is no need to try and control your breath in any way. Simply observe that when you inhale, you relax, and when you exhale, you release all the tension. Inhale and exhale. Pay attention to the natural rhythm of your breath.

Turn your attention to the base of your spine. Picture a beautiful bright red light swirling by your tailbone. It swirls around like a whirlpool. Try to pay attention to how it feels and how it looks. Tune in to how it functions. Try to see its movements. How fast is it moving? Is it fast or slow? Is it a tiny red light or a big light?

Bring your attention back to your breath. You are taking in relaxation and releasing tension: in with relaxation, out with tension.

Now, begin to breathe red light into your root chakra. As you do this, watch that red light begin to grow larger gently. With every inhalation, you are pulling more fresh red light into your root chakra, allowing it to fill and spread out in every direction.

Breathe in this red light energy and breathe out tension: in with the energy and out with the stress.

All of this red light is bringing you strength, security, and health. Allow this red light to fill you as it spreads out and down to your toes.

Feel how empowered you have become as it creates a connection with the energy of the Earth. Feel all of this lovely red light gently encircle you.

You are grounded. You are safe. You are strong.

With every inhalation, you are taking in fresh earthy energy.

With every exhalation, you are releasing old energy.

You breathe in security.

And, you breathe out fear.

You breathe in confidence.

And, you breathe out all of your fears.

You are grounded. You are safe. You are secure.

It is time to begin closing your root chakra.

Turn your attention back to the red light of your root chakra. Visualize it as this light becomes smaller. Allow it to shrink down to the size of fairy light.

In your mind, repeat these words: my root chakra is working as it should; I have created a balanced approach to meet my earthly needs. All of my needs will now be taken care of.

Now, turn your attention back to the flow of your breath, as it moves in and out, in and out.

Notice how cool your breath is as it enters your nose, travels down your throat, and fills your lungs.

Notice how your tummy naturally moves as you take a breath in and release it.

Now, pay attention to your entire body as it rests against your seat.

Feel your toes. Give them a gentle wiggle.

Feel your fingers, and gently wiggle them.

Shrug your shoulders slightly.

Slowly, let yourself to become aware of the room, and all the sounds that are around you.

Once you feel ready, you can open your eyes.

Root Chakra Guided Meditation

Get relaxed in your seated position and take a long, full breath. As you release your breath, turn your attention to the base of your spine. Picture a bright ruby red chakra in your mind. This warm, glowing red light of your chakra calms you, and you begin to feel safe and serene.

You are feeling unshakeable and grounded, like a giant boulder that is cradled by the Earth.

Picture yourself standing at the foot of a high snow-covered mountain that towers over you. Right in front of you is the opening to a large cave.

There are red rhododendrons growing from the mouth of the cave. The breeze causes the flowers to sway gently, and they reflect the beautiful sunlight that is falling on them. The streaks of sun rays at the opening of the cave invite you in.

You walk inside the cave. You look around and see that the cave has high ceilings, and as you rub your hand against the wall, you notice that the walls of the cave are smooth. There is a warm and gentle breeze blowing into the cave, making it quite comfortable and cozy. You continue to walk further into the cave.

The path opens into a large, circular room. At the center, there is a large rectangular stone. There is a crack in the ceiling where a gentle beam of light shines through, bathing the stone in a warm glow.

You walk over to the stone and sat on it. You comfortably cross your legs.

You begin noticing that you feel as if you are a part of this mountain. You feel that you have become deeply rooted and anchored into the Earth. You feel that you are safe. You can feel that the Earth is nourishing and supporting your entire body.

Now, turn your attention to your first chakra. See it spinning and gaining strength. As it continues to spin faster, you become washed in a ruby red light that sinks into every pore and cell in your body.

You take a deep breath and feel all of the energy swirling down to the base of your spine.

You bask in this newfound awareness.

Once you feel your chakra has absorbed all of the energy it needs, you rise from the stone and walk back to the passageway. You walk back out of the cave, stopping to look up the mountain. You still feel completely connected with it.

Once you are ready, open your eyes.

Sacral

Sacral Chakra Clearing Meditation

Get into a comfortable seated position, with your spine straight. Let your forearms rest gently on your legs, with your palms facing up.

Focus into your breathing, and slowly close your eyes.

Breathe, long and slow. Focus on how your breath travels into your lungs.

Slowly release your breath. Focus on this exhalation by picturing your breath as it leaves your body, taking with it all the stress from the day.

Take another deep breath. Picture your breath being pulled all the way into your lungs, and as it moves into your lungs, feel yourself becoming more relaxed, at peace, and comfortable.

Slowly release this breath, focusing on your exhalation.

Picture your breath leaving your body, getting rid of all of the tension, making you feel at peace and relaxed.

Now, slowly shift your focus to your sacral chakra.

Focus on the space that is about two inches below your belly button.

Picture a small ball of light starting to appear in the center of your chakra. It is small, but it is a bright spot.

As you keep your focus to this point, you observe as the light begins to expand. Its dimensions continue to grow larger.

You notice that this ball of light is becoming a radiant orange color.

As you take your next breath, picture your breath being pulled down your spine and then into that glowing orange ball.

With each inhalation, you notice that the ball of orange light grows and expands, becoming brighter and vivid.

You can now see that your sacral chakra is completely open. You can see all the orange energy swirling around like waves, flowing in a clockwise motion.

Watch these vivid orange waves, the vibrancy of your chakra, swirling, radiating, and pulsing to help balance your sacral chakra.

Again, inhale slowly, and focus on your breathing. Watch it. Feel it as it moves through your spine and into your chakra.

Hold your breath for a moment.

Slowly release the breath.

As you release your breath, picture it as a vibrant orange ball moving up your spine and then leaving through your crown.

You become completely aware that as you breathe out, the orange energy waves of your sacral chakra are clearing all of the barriers and blocks you have in your life.

As you bring your sacral chakra into balance, you are getting rid of old emotions and behavioral patterns that no longer serve your higher purpose.

In your next deep breath, watch it as it travels on your spine and into your sacral chakra.

Hold your breath for a moment.

When you release your breath, let it flow out like a stream flowing all the way up to your spine and leaving through your crown.

Again, when you exhale, picture your breath coming from your sacral chakra, an orange ball of energy removing all the blocks and getting rid of any trauma and negative emotions.

Try to sense all of the energy waves from your sacral chakra, getting rid of all the energy blocks that do not serve you anymore.

Take another slow deep breath, focusing on how your breath moves on your back and into your sacral chakra.

Hold.

And then, slowly let your breath out. Watch it flow like a stream up your spine and through your crown.

Picture the breath stream from your sacral chakra as you exhale.

Watch as this orange light of energy clear out all your blocks and get rid of any strain and negative emotions.

Feel all the waves of energy get rid of the energy blocks that do not serve you.

Now, turn your focus back to your sacral chakra.

Watch its vivid orange energy swirling in a clockwise direction.

Picture all the waves of orange energy from your sacral chakra spreading outward, still moving in a clockwise direction.

Watch as these vivid orange energy waves flow and spread wider until they fill your entire body.

Picture all these orange waves swirl and fill your aura.

Watch this beautiful orange energy flowing through your body and filling you. Imagine it filling your aura with all of its cleansing energy.

Repeat these affirmations in your head to yourself.

I adore and love my body.

I am ready to experience the present with all of my senses open and aware.

I am passionate, and I have created healthy boundaries with others

I feel pleasure with every single breath that I take.

I take care of my needs and nourish myself only in ways that are healthy.

I respect and value myself and my body.

Now, slowly bring your attention back to your sacral chakra.

Focus solely on the center point of your chakra and take some time to feel the energy.

Enjoy all of the sensations from your sacral chakra and the orange waves flowing like a waterfall throughout your body. Feel this chakra get rid of everything that you no need. Notice how it nourishes your sense of worth and self.

You can enjoy this and know that your sacral chakra is in balance. You understand why your chakra needs to be in balance.

Once you are done, you can slowly begin taking notice of where you are. Take note of the sounds around you, and then slowly and in your own time, open your eyes. Feel all the sacral energy still within you.

Color Breathing Sacral Chakra Meditation

Get into a comfortable position. If you have chosen to lie down, allow your body to relax on the surface fully. If you are sitting, make sure your back is straight, and your hands are relaxed in your lap.

And, as you shut your eyes, remind yourself that this is your time. Let all of your worries disappear.

Relax yourself into the flow of the moment. Whatever comes easily to you is precisely what you need.

The only thing that exists is right here, right now. The future and the past are not relevant at this moment.

Listen for any sounds that come from the outside, take notice of them, and then let them float away. Listen for any sounds in your surroundings, hear them, and then let them drift away.

Let your body know that it is okay to relax. Feel your legs and soften your feet wherever they are. Feel your shoulders drop down your sides. Let your hands rest.

Let your entire body soften and relax into a natural position.

Feel your face and head relax, your hair and scalp soften, and your forehead flatten. Your eyebrows, eyes, nose, cheeks, chin, jaw, and ears are all softening and relaxing.

Now, take a deep, cleansing breath, and as you release it, let all the stress leave your body.

Let your breath follow a natural rhythm. Do not try to force it in any way. Simply observe your breath bring relaxation and your exhalation release tension. In and out. Watch the natural flow of your breath.

If you find that thoughts are interrupting your practice, allow them to pass through your mind. And then, bring your attention back to your breath, inhaling and exhaling.

Turn your attention to your lower abdomen. Picture a pretty orange light, and watch it swirl like a whirlpool. Take note of how it looks and feels. Try to understand its functions. Is there any tingling there? Do you have any thoughts popping up? How fast is the light swirling? Is it a small light or a big light? Are there any other colors that you see in your mind's eye?

Now, focus your attention back to your breathing.

When you inhale, you are taking in relaxation, and when you exhale, you are releasing anxiety: in with relaxation, out with anxiety.

Now, breathe in the fresh orange light into your sacral chakra. Watch as that orange light begins to grow with every breath you take. In every inhalation, you are pulling more orange light into your sacral chakra. It is filling your chakra and swirling outward, spreading through the rest of your body.

You are inhaling orange light energy and releasing tension: inhale and exhale.

As you continue to breathe in more of this orange light, you begin to feel more creative. You sense fulfillment and happiness. As you release your breath, the orange light removes all of the toxins and blocks in your body.

Allow this orange light to fill your entire being, spreading all the way down your toes and up to your chest and into your body and throughout all of your chakras.

Feel the loveliness of this orange light as it continues to spin and envelope you gently. Let yourself feel emotionally fulfilled. Openly welcome all of the healing pleasures in your life. You are full of creativity.

You breathe in joy and breathe out anger: in with joy, out with anger.

It is now time to close your chakra. Turn your attention back to your lower abdomen and the orange light of your sacral chakra. Picture this light growing smaller. It shrinks down to the size of fairy light. It is returning to its normal function. Tell yourself: my sacral chakra is working as it normally should.

Turn your awareness back to your breath: in and out, in and out.

Feel how cool the air feels as it enters your nose, flows down your throat, and fills your lungs. Notice how your tummy moves naturally with each breath: in and out.

Begin feeling your surroundings and your entire body as it rests on the floor. Turn your attention to your toes. Wiggle them a bit. Focus on your fingers and shake them.

Shrug your shoulders up and down. Be aware of the sounds around you. Finally, open your eyes when you are ready.

Passion Sacral Chakra Meditation

When you are comfortable, take in a long deep breath. As you release your breath, take your attention to your lower abdomen, just below the navel. Picture your glowing orange chakra.

This orange glow starts to spread through the rest of your body; it creates a ripple effect through your body.

You can feel it as it ebbs and flows, like gentle waves crashing on your body.

Picture yourself standing at the edge of a perfect, white-sand beach, just before dawn. There are beautiful orange streaks in the sky, eager for the sun. Watch this sky.

Now, look around at the infinite expanse of the gentle water in front of you. Walk forward, and let the water touch your toes. Notice how the water slowly approaches your ankles and then rushes back out to sea.

You continue to walk forward until the waves are caressing your thighs and knees. The way is crystal clear. You can easily see the white sand under your feet.

You dive into the ocean and effortlessly swim around. You flip onto your back and begin to float in the water, weightlessly.

You watch the orange sky above you, flowing and moving with the waves.

Now, watch as your sacral chakra spins faster and gains more strength. As it continues to spin, you become covered in orange light. It takes over every pore and cell in your body.

Take in a long deep breath and feel all of its energy moving along your spine and into your open chakra.

Relax with this awareness

Now, focus on your swimming again. You notice that the sea has carefully taken you back to the shore, and you are lying on the sand. You begin to walk away from the beach.

You look back to the sea and feel that you have become one with it.

Once you feel ready to return out of this meditation, open your eyes and slowly bring yourself back to your surroundings.

Solar Plexus

Solar Plexus Opening Meditation

Sit in a cross-legged position on the floor and feel the connection between your bones and the floor beneath you. Rooting into the Earth, let your spine drift gently up to the sky, up to the top of your head.

Breathe in, letting your shoulders drop down and softly come to rest. Start becoming aware of the flow of your breath as it moves through your body. You should observe every part of your body. Your body moves gently as you fill it with breath.

You are going to start to stoke your inner fire with your breath by using what is known as the breath of fire. Inhale deeply into your nose, filling your lungs up and then forcefully exhale your breath through the nose, pulling your navel in toward the spine. Continue the process, quickly pumping your belly with the power in your breath.

You cannot do this wrong. Do not judge yourself. Listen to your inner voice and pause this breathing whenever you need to and return once you are ready. As you do this, visualize a bright yellow flame growing larger with each breath you take.

When you are ready, take your breath back to its regular rhythm. Bring your attention to your body and see how you feel, especially within your belly.

Take your hands up to your heart center, with your fingers spread out wide.

Now, bring your fingertips to touch each other, and bring your hands down to hover over your solar plexus chakra. Take your awareness to the palm of your hands and feel all the energy flowing in this area.

During your meditation, set the intention of letting all the energy become a healing force, and ask it to flow into this space, which is the area of your solar plexus chakra.

Start to think of a time when you felt strong in your own power—when you felt completely powerful, driven, and confident. Let this flow through your heart center and ripple out through every part of your body.

Visualize in your core this beautiful, beaming yellow sun that shoots out of your belly, cleansing all of your systems of judgment, fatigue, aggressiveness, and poor self-worth.

Watch this light as it expands and grows more vibrant in color and bigger in size. Watch as it starts to circle and fill your entire body with nourishment, determination, power, and confidence. Ask this light to rise all the way up to the sun.

Picture yourself standing outside on a warm sunny day in your favorite spot in nature. Feel the rays of sun warm your skin. Feel yourself being charged with those rays, your body becoming more and more alive with every single breath.

Now, bring your attention back to your where you are sitting and touching the floor. Root yourself back to the

Earth and then slowly blink your eyes open, coming back to your physical space.

Solar Plexus Meditation

Once you are comfortable, close your eyes and slowly breathe through your nose. Start to become aware of your body and mind and let yourself to relax into the present. This is the only thing you have to focus on.

Feel your body, relax, and soften. Ease your legs and feet. Feel your shoulders drop in relaxation. Let your hand relax, as well. Feel the muscles in your face soften. Your forehead, eyebrows, nose, cheeks, jaw, ear, and scalp are all softening.

As you continue to relax into your meditation, take your awareness to your belly. Lay your hands over your solar plexus chakra, one resting on top of the other.

With your hands in place, start using three-part breathing. We will do this slowly, bit by bit. But, start out breathing in a natural manner completely through your nose. Simply focus on your breath and let your mind to come to rest. Do not entertain any thoughts that come into your mind. Simply let them drift away.

As you enter into your meditative state, start making your breaths longer. Inhale and exhale fully and completely. Make your inhales longer, filling your belly up like a balloon. As you exhale, push the air through your nose with purpose. Make your spine long and pull your navel into your belly to push the last bits of air out.

Inhale again into your belly, filling it up with air. Continue to breathe in deeply, filling and expanding your ribcage and diaphragm. Feel your ribs inflate with your breath.

As you exhale, slowly let the air in your chest out, pulling your lower chest and ribs back together. Then, push the air out of your belly.

With your next breath, slowly inhale and expand your diaphragm and belly just a little more than the last time and let it fill your upper chest.

Feel the air expand all the way up to your collar and heart. Feel all those areas expanding.

As you breathe out, slowly allow the air to come out of your upper chest, lower chest, diaphragm, and your belly. Continue this type of breathing as you go on with your meditation.

As you breathe, connect with the energy around and inside you, especially your solar plexus. Imagine the energy of this chakra inside of you as a radiant ball of yellow light. Feel its warmth pulse through your body and observe how it feels. Is it weak or strong? Does it move? Focus on all of this energy.

With every breath, start tapping into this energy and light. What do you want from this energy? Start to feel your strength and confidence, and feel it grow strong with each breath.

As you sit with this energy, take a deep breath, and ignite the energy of your solar plexus, just as if you had lit a match. Hold this and release your breath and allow the energy to spread through each of your cells. Every part of your body is wrapped in this yellow glow and warmth. Imagine that you have accomplished the purpose you have set.

Repeat these affirmations to yourself:

I am resilient, energized, and filled with my own physical power. I am worthy of being listened to, respected, and loved. I am happy, confident, and proud of myself. I accept and deserve the life that I want. I choose to move toward my dreams.

Hold onto these feelings and emotions that these affirmations have created in your body.

Once you are ready to come out of this meditation, take your hands up to the center of your chest in the prayer mudra, and bow your head. Bring your awareness back into your body. Take another deep breath, and then open your eyes.

Heart

Meditation to Open the Heart Chakra

This meditation is the best way you can become present with awareness and intelligence. Studies have shown that the intelligence of the heart, emotional intelligence, is a lot more receptive to the truth of your outer and inner life than your mind. Thoughts going through your mind are constantly changing, but your heart's knowledge is rooted in a more in-depth type of intelligence. It is more intuitive.

Let us begin.

Be still and give your heart the attention it needs and wants.

Find your meditation spot and get comfortable. Soften your eyes, let your mind relax, make your spine long, elongate your neck, and bring your shoulders down to relax them. Keep your eyes closed and start to focus on your breathing. With every breath, let all the tension in your body go. With your mind's eye, scan your whole body and find where the tension resides. Focus your breathing into that part and let the tension in these places dissolve with every breath.

Deliberately allow yourself to feel extremely relaxed. Now, put your awareness on your heart chakra. How does this space in your body feel? Do you feel any contraction, anxiety, or tension? If you find any of these, allow your breath to move into your heart chakra. Summon it to feel extremely relaxed, secure, and safe.

Just take notice of any sensations you may be feeling around your heart chakra. It may feel free from stress and open. You may feel an energy blockage. It may be heavy or light. Whatever you feel, just let it be. Simply let it be there. Send it some loving thought just like you would a child you love.

Visualize every nourishing and nurturing breath you take; you are getting rid of all the dust and dirt that is covering your heart. Visualize that your breath is going into your heart and leaving through your heart. Remain here with your breathing for several minutes.

Do you feel as if your heart is opening and softening some more? If you don't, take more time to breathe in and out of your heart chakra. You can pause here and ask your heart some questions if you like. See how different the answers are as compared to the answers if you had asked your brain these questions instead. Continue to breathe and remain in this awareness for several minutes.

Once you are ready, slowly open your eyes. Place your hands into the prayer position over your heart. Give your heart a bow and tell it you will join it soon. Say "thank you" for its guidance and wisdom. Now, you may go about your daily activities.

Heart Chakra Meditation

This chakra is located near your heart. It controls your ability to receive and give love, reach out to others, and feel compassion. It is in the middle of all the chakras in your body, and it balances all the chakras. It is the chakra that links the lower ones to the higher ones. It holds joy, compassion, warmth, and love. It helps you create deep bonds with yourself, as well as increasing your generosity, altruism, and other emotional things. It helps you know that you are part of more significant things and that you are connected in a web of relationships that extend out to the Universe and life itself.

Let us begin.

Lie down or get into a comfortable position. You can use props, blankets, and bolsters as needed for you to get relaxed and comfortable. Relax your whole body. Sink onto the mat underneath you. Starting at your feet, relax your body. Now, move from your feet to the ankles, calves, knees, and thighs. Take notice of your whole leg, and make sure they are relaxed. Feel the ground supporting you. Move the relaxation to your bottom, lower back, middle back, upper back, and shoulders. Make any adjustments to your position in order to relax your body further. Now, relax your upper arms, elbows, forearms, and hands. Release any tension you may be holding in these parts. Make sure that your shoulders are in complete contact with the mat. Release any tension from your face. Soften the muscles around your forehead and eyes. Relax your jaw. Let your mouth to open a little bit so that your jaws are not touching.

Now, move your awareness inward, and begin to focus on your breathing. Put your hand over your belly and the other one over your chest near your heart. Be aware of your body moving with each breath. Let your body breathe at a normal pace.

Now, we are going to say some affirmations together. You can choose to repeat them to yourself, or just focus your attention inward. Affirmations are just messages for your subconscious. So, even if you're asleep, you will still get some benefits from them. You can visualize yourself planting affirmations like seeds in loving, supportive, fertile soil in your heart. Visualize these seeds being nurtured with love as they grow into beautiful, luscious, vibrant, flower, vines, and plants.

Repeat each one twice, slowly.

"I remain quiet and listen to my heart sing."

"I choose to be united with all beings, whether they are invisible or visible, in the realm of light and love."

"Love can open and heal me."

"I choose the peace that surpasses all understanding."

"I am love. I am in peace. I am light."

"I follow my heart's desire for truth, goodness, and love."

"My core is innocent and pure. Nothing can touch the soul of my heart except love itself."

"I open my heart to everything that is good."

"Joy is the reason I continue to live."

"I look for joy in myself, and I see it in everything."

"I allow my heart to shine and give it from the depth of my being to the people who accept love."

"I am worth loving. There is love all around me."

"I open my heart and sing the joys of love."

Be aware of how your heart is responding to these words of love. The seeds you have planted will grow tall and strong will all your loving energy and support to the garden in your heart.

Now that you have planted a garden of loving thoughts in your mind, I want for you to set an intention now. By using a mantra, visualization, pranayama, and asana, you can harness your mind and send vibrations to your spirit to convey its message. You may want to set an intention for mindfulness, spiritual expansion, or connection. You may set an intention of love, inner peace, or bliss as well. Setting intentions instead of goals needs to be the way of our life.

Now, visualize this. See what it feels like to find a bright white orb that is hovering over you. Squeeze this orb into a powerful, tiny pearl that is shining and opalescent. Plant this "seed" in your heart's garden. You need to feed this seed with compassion and love, nurture it, care for it, and let it grow tall and strong. It buds with flowers that are red and bright pink.

Now, I want you to visualize a green sphere or a cloth that drapes over your shoulders that illuminates your chest and heart with a green light. Breathe in. Watch as this light gets brighter and fuller of love. When you breathe out, this green energy light will radiate through your spine and through your whole body. It is filling each cell of your body with love that is perfect. This green light is bathing your whole body. It begins to spiral, building speed. Finally, your heart opens and blooms with beautiful shades of green like flowers in springtime. Let this light expand from your body to the area around you, your room, house, neighborhood, town, state, country, and the entire planet. Send this healing light to anyone who needs it the most. Slowly visualize this green light coming back to you. Take a few minutes to celebrate in this wonderful garden you planted in your heart. Enjoy it; show gratitude for how you are feeling right this very minute. Enjoy all the scents and colors of this beautiful ecosystem you built in your heart. Know that you can come to this place anytime you like. It will always be inside of you.

As you leave this meditation practice, slowly wake up your body. Move your toes and fingers; bring your awareness to where you are. Take a big breath and stretch your arms as far as you can. Stretch your legs. Deeply yawn to activate your nervous system. Now, exhale and feel the energy coming to you. Hug your knees to your chest. You could also roll into the fetal position, lying on your side with your head propped on your arm if you want to.

When you are ready, you may get up and resume your daily activities.

Throat

Throat Chakra Meditation

This meditation will activate your throat chakra. This chakra controls how well you can express yourself and how you communicate with the world. Its element is space. Its Sanskrit name is Vishuddha, which means purity.

Let us begin.

Take some deep breaths to help calm your mind and body. Shut your eyes slowly.

Take another deep breath. Inhale until your lungs are completely full and your stomach has expanded. Now, release all the air from your lungs. Bring your awareness to your throat and visualize that your chakra is blue like a sapphire. This blue glow pulses from your throat, fills your neck and head, and then moves through your entire body.

Visualize that you are walking through a forest. There is a narrow path that has huge trees on both sides that give a nice shade. You hear insects and small animals scurrying through the undergrowth. You hear happy birds chirping in the trees overhead. You can hear a stream rushing in the distance.

You get to a clearing and see a huge tree that has fallen onto the forest floor. You walk toward it and sit down on the ground with your back against this tree.

The sounds around you become clearer; they have a magical quality. You realize you can hear even the smallest sound. The entire forest is playing you a symphony.

You realize that your throat chakra is spinning faster and gaining strength. While it begins to spin faster, the sapphire blue light washes over you and spreads to every pore and cell within your body.

Take another deep breath and feel this energy pouring into your throat. Your throat is bursting with this beautiful blue light.

Take a few minutes and rest in awareness.

Slowly stand and begin to walk away from this fallen tree to the forest you just emerged from. Turn around and look at this forest. Hear the music and be one with it.

Once you are ready, you may open your eyes, and go back to your tasks.

Throat Chakra Color Breathing Meditation

This meditation helps you open and activate your throat chakra by visualizing the color blue.

Let us begin.

The first thing you should do is to get comfortable. You can either choose to sit or lie down. Whatever you decide to do, just make sure you are very comfortable. If you are sitting, you can either place your arms at your sides or on your lap, whatever feels most comfortable.

Close your eyes. This moment is yours; leave any worries outside your meditation space. Let yourself relax at this moment. What comes the easiest for you is what is right for you. There isn't anything here that is wrong. There is only this moment. The past or future do not exist in this time and place.

If you hear any sounds outside this room, acknowledge them, and allow them to pass. If you hear anything inside the room, acknowledge it and allow it to pass.

Allow your body to relax; allow your legs and feet to soften. Lower your shoulders, relax your hands, and let your entire body to relax and soften into a natural position. Now, allow your face and head to relax. Let your hair and scalp relax. Your forehead, eyebrows, eyes, nose, cheeks, chin, jaw, and ears must all be relaxed and soft.

Inhale a deep, cleansing breath. When you exhale, make sure you release all the tension from your body.

Let your breath get into a natural rhythm by itself; do not try to control it. Just observe while you are breathing in relaxation and breathing out all the tension: inhale, exhale. Be aware of your breathing's natural rhythm.

If thoughts try to intrude, let them flow past your mind. Bring your attention back to your breath. Inhale, exhale.

Repeat this a few times.

Now, let your awareness come to your throat. Visualize a blue light there, swirling like a whirlpool. Create a mental image of the way it looks and feels. Figure out how it functions. Do you feel any tingling? If there are thoughts coming into your head, what are they? How fast is the light swirling? Is the light big or small? Do you see any other colors?

Visualize the blue light one more time in your throat. Watch it as the glow begins to get larger while it spins.

Once again, let your awareness reside on your breathing. Focus as you inhale and exhale. Repeat this several times. As you breathe, imagine that you are breathing this blue light into your throat. With each intake of air, you are pulling in more and more of this blue light. You let it fill your throat chakra and your entire neck. Watch in your mind's eye as it spreads throughout your whole body. Inhale this blue light into your chest. Inhale it into your arms all the way down to your hands. Inhale it into your stomach, pelvis, legs, and feet. Now, imagine you are breathing this blue light into your warmth, allowing it to fill up. Observe as this blue light connects all the chakras.

While breathing in this blue light, it will bring you good listening skills, clear expression, and the truth.

As you breathe out, this blue light will remove every blockage that exists in your body. Feel this blue light as it spins and encompasses you. Inhale the blue light, and exhale tension. Tell yourself you are expressive, truthful, and transparent. Inhale the blue light, and exhale negativity. Repeat this a few more times.

Visualize this spinning blue light and watch as it opens like a twirling flower that gets larger. Notice the energy and light of the Divine pouring guidance to your hearing, mind, and entire body. It is enlightening each cell in your being. Keep this image in your mind for as long as you can.

Now, bring your awareness to your chest area. See the green light of your heart chakra. Observe the swirling blue light getting smaller and smaller until it is a spot. Bring it back to normal function. Repeat this: "My throat chakra functions well."

Bring your mind back to the breathing exercise. Inhale and exhale. Take note of your breath; it feels fresh as it enters your nose, travels down your throat, and inflates your lungs. Be aware of the normal movement of your stomach while breathing. Inhale and exhale. Picture your entire body once again where it is resting. Be aware of your toes; move them just a bit. Now, move your fingers, and exercise your shoulders. Be mindful of the room you are in; hear any sounds around you. Once you feel ready to move, open your eyes, and end the exercise.

Third Eye

Opening the Third-Eye Meditation

This chakra is located between your eyebrows. When you open this chakra, you can open your senses to be aware of high-dimensional energies and worlds.

If you like the ability to see another person's angels or auras or even your own energies, you have to learn how to open this center. You cannot do this to impress anyone. This skill is important as it can enrich and change your life.

Your third eye is the center of clairvoyant sight. It refers to the ability to perceive or see all these subtle energies. Some people call it "sixth sense," which means you acquire the capability to access impressions that go beyond the normal five senses.

Let us begin.

Find a place where you will be comfortable and won't be disturbed. Avoid tight clothes, dim the lights if they are very bright, and close the curtains.

Start this meditation slowly. Allow yourself a lot of time to get settled to make the experience deeper.

Start by taking a deep breath and hold it. Now, exhale gently through your mouth. Notice how you automatically relax as you breathe.

Separate your jaws to relax your face. Take note of how your whole body relaxed just a bit more.

Let this relaxation spread through your body deeply. Allow it to relax you even more.

Now, bring your awareness to the area right between the eyebrows. Be aware of your third eye. This is the energy area in your forehead. It is radiating light and beginning to open. Visualize a golf-ball sized golden light radiating light around you in every direction.

Get rid of all your thoughts, resistance, uncertainty, anxiety, or fear that this isn't going to work for you. You can do this just by finding the places of resistance and taking a deep breath and exhaling out all of it.

This process is natural and safe. The ball of golden light will put you in a frequency where positive experiences can happen. Only positive experiences can happen here. All you have to do is relax, and let it happen.

Allow this ball of light on your forehead to open up and send golden glow to every direction, allowing it to soothe you more.

Let your body become more relaxed.

Notice that you are getting lighter as more light flows from your third eye to the rest of your body.

Let yourself release all uncertainty and questions.

Allow yourself to let this chakra to open by itself naturally. You will feel more relaxed, and the chakra will open as well.

This process is completely natural. Allow your mind to get rid of all ideas on what you think will happen.

Now would be a good time to call on your spirit guides or angels and ask for support. Ask them to help you do what you don't know how to do. Allow them to help you open this chakra.

Let the golden ball of light constantly flow through you and out of this chakra. Open this golden ball of light into an expanse of clear, pure light over your head, and allow this light to become purer and brighter.

Now, connect your higher self and soul. Ask that it fills you with pure golden light. Let it fill your aura and body; let it travel around you.

Ask if your spirit guide has any message about opening your third eye. Pause for a few minutes to see if you get any messages.

Ask what you should know or need to do to open your third eye. What has to happen?

See if there are any visions, impressions, images, or thoughts that come into your mind.

It may feel as if you are using your imagination or just daydreaming. You may think that you are just making it up. In time, you will realize that you are receiving energy impressions. Follow these impressions to the other worlds, and they will unfold to you.

Once you feel that you have meditated long enough, gently bring your awareness back into the present. Become aware of your legs, arms, hands, and body.

Repeat after me. "I am fully present in the now."

Take a deep breath, stretch, and commit to yourself that you are going to continue doing this third-eye meditation.

Third-Eye Meditation

This meditation will help you activate your third-eye chakra. This chakra controls your visualization, imagination, and intellect. It has the element of light. It means command. Its Sanskrit name is Ajna.

Let us begin.

Take some deep breaths to calm your mind and body; close your eyes.

Take a deep, long breath. While you are exhaling, bring your mind on your forehead, right between your eyebrows and a little bit above your brow line. Visualize a chakra that is indigo in color. This color will light up your mind and spread throughout your body.

Visualize that there is an entrance to your mind through your third eye. Watch yourself open this door and go into an empty room. You have the freedom to decorate this room how you like. You get to choose the feel, look, décor, and color.

Be sure that it suits your taste so it can become your sanctuary.

Now, walk around this room, and find the most comfortable spot where you can sit down.

Look out into the world from this spot. Focus on the same ideas, situations, issues, and thoughts that occupy your daily life. Sit and silently think about them.

Now, watch as this chakra spins and gains strength. As this chakra spins faster and faster, the indigo light spreads through every pore and cell in your body.

Inhale deeply and feel this energy bursting from your third eye like rays of beautiful blue light.

Take a few minutes, and just bask in this awareness.

Now, slowly stand up and walk over to the door. Open this door, walk out, and turn around to look at your inner sanctuary, feeling a connection with it.

When you are ready, you may open your eyes, and come back to the present.

Crown

Crown Chakra Meditation

This meditation will help activate your seventh chakra or your crown chakra. This chakra controls your cerebral cortex. This is responsible for helping you get to a "higher state of consciousness" or "another world."

There isn't an element associated with this chakra, but some like to refer to the "mind" or "thoughts" as its element.

In Sanskrit, the name for this chakra is Sahasrara. This word means "one thousand." Its symbol is the "thousand-petaled lotus."

Let us begin the meditation.

Start by taking some deep breaths to calm your mind and body. Close your eyes.

Take another deep breath. Fill your lungs completely, expanding your stomach as you breathe. Now, exhale and bring your awareness to the very topmost part of your head and try to picture a purple glow. This color glows brightly and lights up your body and mind.

Now, visualize a huge white lotus; its petals are closed, and it is sitting where your crown chakra is located. Look at this lotus, and think about its texture, color, and shape.

While you are staring at this lotus, it begins to swirl; your chakra begins to swirl, too.

The petals open one by one. Once the first layer of petals has opened, you notice that there are more and more rows that still need to be opened.

With each new layer of petals that open, the lotus begins to spin faster and faster. You see that each opening just leads to another layer of petals. The blooming lotus is a process that has infinite stages.

Now, visualize your chakra spinning at the same speed as the lotus. The violet light completely washes over you and spreads throughout every pore and cell of your body.

Take a deep breath and feel the energy from this chakra connecting you to the universe and the earth underneath you. You realize that you are connected to everything, and you have become one with the universe.

Take some time to rest. Bask in this new awareness…

Once you are done, you may open your eyes and get up.

Meditation to Heal the Chakras

This meditation will take you on a journey that will restore energy and cleanse your chakras. It will bring your whole energy system into balance and harmony.

Let us start.

Close your eyes and become aware of your breathing. Become aware of your body; fee your mind and belly softening with each breath.

Feel the floor below you, connecting you to the ground below. Allow it to take your weigh.

Take note of the shade and light and the air that is touching your body.

You can sense the sky above, the horizon that stretches around you, and the earth that supports you.

Empty your mind of things it does not need. Just let them go. Allow it to flow away. Let your body release what it does not need. Just let it go; allow it to drift away.

Bring yourself back; bring your energy to your center. Ground yourself in the present.

Start opening your senses to your surroundings. Breathe deeply while being mindful of the rise and fall of your chest. It comes, and it goes. Notice the temperature, sound, and sensation around you.

Breathe down into your body weight, into your root chakra, and underneath your spine. Remind yourself that this is the chakra of belonging. Be mindful of this chakra as you take a breath. Soften it with gentle breaths. Bask in the life force energy and nourishment it provides.

Let this chakra connect you to the ground below. Let it travel beneath the earth. Bring in the red color, as it is the Earth's hue. Immerse your root chakra in this energy; allow it to ground, embody, and empower you. Allow the chakra to take everything it needs. And, say these motivations: "I am here." "I am alive, with the right to be where I am." "The Earth has an endless bounty that supports me."

And when you are done, move your focus to your stomach, below your belly button. This is the chakra of pleasure, movement, creativity, choice, and emotional intelligence.

Breathe into this chakra; allow it to expand and soften with each breath. Take in the energy you require, as well as the nourishment and life force you need. Now, visualize the color orange, like the setting sun. Bathe your chakra with orange; allow it to motivate, empower, and balance the chakra. Feed your chakra this energy and repeat these words: "I know my necessities and honor them." "I deserve to be nourished."

After this, move your consciousness on your belly where your solar plexus chakra resides. Breathe in, expanding and kindling your chakra, which governs your personal power. Breathe in and out. Use your mind's eye to see yellow, like the sun's rays. It is the color of the solar plexus. Immerse your chakra in the sunshine to energize it.

Let it nurture, restore, and replenish you. Allow this chakra to take everything it needs. Say these inspirations. "I am more than enough." "I honor and give value to my well-being." "I am worth my weight in gold."

After this, focus your energy into your heart chakra. This is the chakra of unconditional love and self-development.

Breathe into your heart chakra. Let this chakra expand and soften with every breath. Imagine a rose-pink glow or the color green, whatever you like. Bathe your heart chakra with your chosen color. Bring in healing, renewal, and nourishment; allow it to take everything. Say these affirmations to yourself: "I am greatly loved." "I allow myself to give and receive love freely." "I am nourished by the power of love."

When done, focus your mind's eye on your neck or throat chakra. This is the chakra of personal will and self-expression.

Let this chakra expand and soften with every breath. Imagine the color of the sky. Breathe in the color blue and send it to your throat chakra to soften and open it. Forget the need to be in control; let it free your creativity and self-expression. Allow it to absorb everything and affirm yourself with these words: "I perceive the truth and express my truth." "My self-expression is free." "I accept the natural flow of life."

When you are done, bring your focus between your eyebrows, and try to envision your third-eye chakra. This is the chakra of intuition and wisdom. Allow it to expand and soften with each breath you take. Imagine the color indigo, the color of the night sky. Bathe the third eye in this color. Bring in understanding, insight, clarity, balance, and soothing. Let your third-eye chakra absorb everything and express these affirmations: "Everything is unfolding the way it should."

When you are done meditating with your third-eye chakra, imagine your crown chakra. Focus on the crown of your head in this exercise. This is the chakra of oneness; allow it to expand and soften with each breath you take. Envision the color purple and bathe your crown chakra with this color. Invite harmony, restoration, and balance. Let your chakra absorb everything. Say your affirmations: "I am attuned with the Universe." "I am part of the Whole."

If you feel it is enough, let your consciousness move to your body. Go back to your breathing and perform the breathing exercise once more. Say these motivations: "I am whole." "I am who I am, and I am perfect." Let these words give you energy and immerse your body, spirit, emotions, and mind, and body.

If you feel you are done meditating, bring your awareness to the air you feel on your body and the sounds around you.

Now, close all your chakras one by one. Bring awareness to the ground beneath you and your surroundings. Observe your feelings, be aware of yourself, and appreciate your uniqueness and beauty.

End this meditation practice when you are ready.

Conclusion

Clearing and unblocking your chakras will do amazing things for your mind and body. Working with these meditations each day will ensure that your chakras remain unblocked.

As mentioned, a lot of negative things can happen if you leave your chakras blocked. Nobody wants to face physical and mental disruptions when they can be easily fixed.

It is essential that you establish a routine for your chakra practice. This will ensure that you never forget to do it and that your chakras will function to the best of their abilities.

FREE BONUS

P.S. Is it okay if we overdeliver?

I believe in overdelivering way beyond our reader's expectations. Is it okay if I overdeliver?

Here's the deal, I am going to give you an extremely valuable cheatsheet of "Accelerated Learning"…

What's the catch? I need to trust you… You see, my team and I wants to overdeliver and in order for us to do that, we've to trust our reader to keep this bonus a secret to themselves. Why? Because we don't want people to be getting our ultimate accelerated learning cheatsheet without even buying our books itself. Unethical, right?

Ok. Are you ready?

Simply Visit this link:
http://bit.ly/acceleratedcheatsheet

Everything else will be self explanatory after you've visited:
http://bit.ly/acceleratedcheatsheet

We hope you'll enjoy our free bonuses as much as we've enjoyed preparing it for you!

The Tales Behind the
Tunes of Glory

The Inspiration for our
Best-Known Pipe Music

With Best Wishes!

Retold and Illustrated by
Stuart Gordon Archer

Stuart Archer

HISTORY AND TRADITIONS OF SCOTLAND SERIES

DEESIDE BOOKS, BALLATER

Published by Deeside Books,
18-20 Bridge Street,
Ballater,
Aberdeenshire AB35 5QP
Tel. 01339 754080
Email: deesidebk@aol.com
Web: www.deesidebooks.com

ISBN: 978-1-90-781310-8

HISTORY AND TRADITIONS OF SCOTLAND SERIES:
1. The Tales Behind the Tunes of Glory by Stuart Gordon Archer.

NORTH-EAST SCOTLAND CLASSICS:
1. Lochnagar by Alex Inkson McConnochie.
2. Loch Kinnord by The Rev. John Grant Michie.
3. Donside by Alex Inkson McConnochie.
4. Aberdeen Street Names by G. M. Fraser.
5. Strathspey by Alex Inkson McConnochie.
6. Ben Muich Dhui and his Neighbours
   by Alex Inkson McConnochie.
7. The Old Deeside Road Revisited by G. J. Marr.
8. The Mounth Passes by G. J. Marr.

Also published or distributed by Deeside Books –
Plant & Roots: A Social History of Ballater by Ian Cameron.
Scenery of the Dee by Jim Henderson.

Printed and bound by Robertsons Printers, Forfar.

*This book is for my mother, Aileen,
from her loving and devoted son.*

The Lairig Ghru from Aviemore

Foreword

Pipe tunes are often as remarkable for their names as for their melodies, and certainly for pipers, their names will instantly summon up the tunes. Beyond the reference to event or person, we have to imagine the rest. But the stories behind pipe tunes should be part of our national memory, not as glorifying war but as remembering events which the piper-composer wanted to commemorate for his own and following generations and such circumstances in which our forebears might have fought and died.

Good music thrives, survives and travels and Stuart Archer is to be congratulated for finding the stories behind the tunes and for keeping in our minds and imagination what has sparked and sustained composition.

The Great Highland Bagpipe has been regarded as an instrument that has inspired the soldier and warfare has given rise to many of the items in this collection, whether the events belonged to the home-brewed Jacobite wars or to the wider wars of empire or horrors of world wars. Even here though, there may be more elegy than eulogy. *The Bloody Fields of Flanders* is perhaps an outstanding example of the importance of chronicling these tragedies, since the old soldier, John McLellan of Dunoon, who witnessed these events, turned his musical genius to commemorate this in such a way as to then later inspire Hamish Henderson's *Freedom Come All Ye*.

This is a richly varied collection of music, artfully bound together by our storyteller who is the 'keeper of records' – the seanchaidh – for future generations of pipers and students of Scottish history (the Gaelic word seanchaidh is pronounced phonetically as shannachy).

Professor Hugh Cheape

Sabhal Mor Ostaig
Oilthigh na Gaidhealtachd agus nan Eilean
An Lunastal 2019.

National Centre for the Gaelic Language and Culture
University of the Highlands and Islands
August 2019.

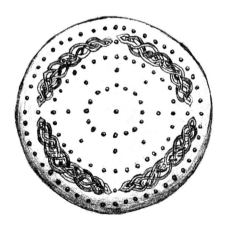

Highland Targe (or Shield)

Preface

This wee book is for anyone who has ever been inspired by the skirl of the pipes.

I hope to demonstrate to you that the history behind pipe tunes is as fascinating as the music is inspiring. Just imagine all the events and colourful characters that have gone before and have provided Scotland with its rich history, culture and music.

Even though many of us enjoy pipe music, there are a bewildering number of tunes, and then tunes that sound a bit like other tunes! Sometimes the titles and the time signatures can appear impenetrable. This book offers a handy reference for some of your favourites whilst providing an insight into the origin of the music and the reasons why the songs were written in the first place.

My interest in Scottish history has been longstanding, but my interest in pipe tune history really started upon learning that there were tune names such as *The 10th Battalion Highland Light Infantry Crossing the Rhine!* Why was MacPherson ranting, and Lord Lovat lamenting? What or where are *The Haughs o' Cromdale*, and can you eat them? I just couldn't play the tunes without knowing more about these weird and wonderful titles. Furthermore, did you know that there have been quite a few contenders for the Scottish National Anthem? This book reveals the background to the most popular, from *Scots Wha Hae* to *Highland Cathedral*.

This is not a history book, but the thirty tunes chosen have been organised chronologically, either in the order that the historical events happened or when the compositions were written. Each story can be read as a separate entity, but if read cover to cover then it should provide a window into Scotland's history, with piping as the common thread.

If you are a piper, you might not know the history behind some of the pipe tunes that you have been playing for years. This guide may be helpful, because knowing even a wee bit about the origin of the pipe tunes should enhance your appreciation of the music. Enjoy reading the background behind the numbers in your repertoire and the next time you play your pipes try to feel the true meaning of a composition rather than just mechanically playing the notes – I guarantee you'll play it all the better!

I love storytelling, and music. This book combines these passions and tries to demonstrate that song is still one of the most powerful ways to communicate and preserve our rich history. This light-hearted offering was compiled from multiple sources and although I have attempted to cross reference to check facts and figures, I am neither a military historian nor an expert in song provenance and so any errors or inaccuracies are apologised for in advance and are mine alone.

These short stories were just waiting to be retold in the form of a collection of strong Scottish narratives. So, if like me you don't really enjoy surfing the interweb-hairnet thingy and prefer a good book, then light the fire, pour a dram, and flick through this easy to read offering.

Stuart Gordon Archer
Dinnet
Aberdeenshire
November 2019.

Contents

Cabar Feidh

Cabar Feidh is a rousing and manic battle tune. Regimental onsets, or charging tunes, are often lively, and *Cabar Feidh* (the Deer's Antlers in Gaelic) is the most famous onset of them all. Although most pipe bands play this as a march with a 4/4 time signature (simple time with four crotchet beats in every bar), it also makes a pleasantly pointed and jerky strathspey.

Clan legend tells that King Alexander III of Scotland was hunting in the Forest of Mar when he was unhorsed by an infuriated stag that had been harassed by his hounds. As the stag attacked, an Irishman called Colin Fitzgerald came to the King's aid by yelling "Cuidich'n Righ" (Help the King) and plunged his spear into the stag behind its antlers, although other storytellers say he lopped off the stag's head!

Alexander III gave land near Eilean Donan in Kintail to Colin for saving his life and for his help in defeating King Haakon of Norway at the Battle of Largs in 1263, the last Viking battle on Scottish soil. Colin Fitzgerald died fifteen years later in 1278. The name of his purported grandson, the 3rd Baron of Kintail, who in Gaelic was called Coinnich MacCoinnich (Kenneth son of Kenneth), became corrupted into MacKenzie in its English form. The name MacKenzie therefore derives from the Gaelic name MacCoinnich, meaning Son of the Fair One. The chiefs of the clan are still addressed as Cabar Feidh, derived from the stag's head crest from the old Mackenzie coat of arms.

The 78th (Highland) Regiment of the British Army had associations with Clan MacKenzie, and the tune *Cabar Feidh* became their regimental march. The 78th were most well known for their involvement in the Siege of Lucknow in 1857, where eight Ross-shire Buffs were awarded the Victoria Cross (VC) between July and September 1857. Their deeds were commemorated by poets such as John Greenleaf Whittier and Alfred, Lord Tennyson. During the Battle of Cawnpore Major-General Havelock addressed his captains:

"I have been forty years in the service.
I have been engaged in action about seven-and-twenty times;
but in the whole of my career
I have never seen any regiment behave better, nay more,
I have never seen anyone behave so well,
as the 78th Highlanders this day.

I am not a Highlander, but I wish I was one".

In 1881, under the Childers Reforms, the 78th Highlanders were amalgamated with the 72nd Highlanders to form the Seaforth Highlanders. The 72nd formed the 1st Battalion (The Duke of Albany's) and the 78th formed the 2nd Battalion (Ross-shire Buffs). The motto Cuidich'n Righ (Help the King) was on the cap badge of the Seaforth Highlanders.

Regimental Cap Badge
of the
Seaforth Highlanders
(1881-1961)

In more modern times, the Seaforth Highlanders merged with the Queen's Own Cameron Highlanders in 1961 to form the Queen's Own Highlanders and in 1994, the Queen's Own Highlanders (Seaforths and Camerons) were amalgamated with the Gordon Highlanders to form The Highlanders. Since 2006, following further rationalisation, these units now make up the 4th Battalion of the Royal Regiment of Scotland (4 SCOTS).

The earliest record of *Cabar Feidh* is in Scottish musician David Young's manuscript of 1734, also known as the Drummond Castle Manuscript. The tune itself may first have been written for the fiddle but didn't appear as a pipe tune until one hundred years later. This popular melody has long been a mainstay of Scottish tradition, but it also entered the Irish tradition where the song *Rakish Paddy* appears to be the closest derivation.

Caber Feidh is a tune with a rare quality in that it lends itself to being played in a number of time signatures and has been interpreted in multiple ways, so there are many variants. To this day, the tune is popular as an accompaniment to highland dances in strathspey and reel time. Highland dancers symbolically replicate the shape of deer's antlers with their arms and fingers (with the thumb and middle finger touching).

Scots Wha Hae

Scots Wha Hae (Scots Who Have) is an old patriotic slow air. It's a popular composition to learn on the chanter as a first tune. This is because it requires easy to learn slow fingerwork, but once proficient a piper can choose to play *Scots Wha Hae* faster at march time. The tune served for a long time as an unofficial national anthem of the country, but it was replaced by *Scotland the Brave* and more recently by *Flower of Scotland*.

Robert Burns (1759-96) is credited with the words, which he penned in 1793. Burns composed the verse as his interpretation of the address that Robert the Bruce gave to his troops before the Battle of Bannockburn in 1314 (the tune has been alternatively called *Bruce's Address*). He makes reference in the first line to the continuity of troops who had fought in the service of William Wallace (wi' Wallace bled) and Robert the Bruce (Bruce has aften led):

> Scots, wha hae wi' Wallace bled,
> Scots, wham Bruce has aften led,
> Welcome tae yer gory bed,
> Or tae victorie.

Burns wrote the words to *Scots Wha Hae* to the old Scottish tune *Hey Tuttie Tatie* (this title is supposed to imitate a trumpet) which, according to tradition, was played by Bruce's army at the Battle of Bannockburn. Following the Scottish Wars of Independence, the tune was then exported to France by Scottish archers who joined the Franco-Scots army at the close of the Hundred Years' War. The Scots, about six thousand strong, were led by John Stewart, the Earl of Buchan, and took a strong military role in France from 1421.

Joan of Arc was led into the besieged city of Orléans on 29th April 1429 to the unmistakable skirl of the Scottish pipes! The tune played for her by the Scots was *Hey Tuttie Tatie* (which was the same tune that had marched Robert the Bruce into battle just over a century before). Around one quarter of the army is estimated to have been made up of Scots.

The relief of Orléans was the watershed in the Hundred Years' War between France and England. It was the French Royal Army's first major military victory following the crushing defeat at the Battle of Agincourt in 1415, and also the first while Joan of Arc was with the army. The tune was also played in Rheims for the coronation of the French King (Charles VII) in July of 1429, where his bodyguard was made up of Scottish forces (Garde Ecossaise). Famously, Joan of Arc was tried as a heretic and on 30th May 1431 was burned at the stake at Rouen. She was later to be declared innocent of all charges and designated a martyr.

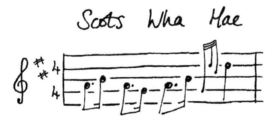

Scots Wha Hae can be danced to as a Scottish waltz if the tempo is chosen well. It is still played in France today where it is known as the *Marche des Soldats de R. Bruce*. As a basis for other songs it also served as a Jacobite carousing song, from 1718, called *Fill up your Bumpers High*, and an Annandale collected song called *Bridekirk's Hunting*.

The Bonnie Lass of Fyvie

This is an upbeat and spirited 4/4 march. It makes a great early learning tune that allows the novice player to focus on their throw on D aptitude. The throw on the D is one of the most important finger movements for a piper to master.

The Bonnie Lass of Fyvie is a Scottish folk song about a thwarted romance between an Irish soldier and a local girl from Fyvie in the north of Aberdeenshire. The narration is in the third person, through the voice of one of the captain's soldiers. The captain promises the girl material comfort and happiness, but Peggy refuses his advances, stating she has no intention of marrying a soldier. The captain, who was named Ned, subsequently leaves Fyvie and dies (presumably of a broken heart or battle wounds or perhaps both?) after dallying in Aberdeenshire for a while. It is possible that the song refers to the period in history surrounding the capture of Fyvie Castle by Montrose's Royalist Army in 1644, as a large proportion of this army was Irish.

Fyvie Castle "The perfect imperfect castle"

There once was a troop o' Irish dragoons,
Cam' marchin' doon through Fyvie-o,
The captain fell in love wi' a very bonnie lass,
And her name it was ca'd pretty Peggy-o.

Now there's many a bonnie lass in the Howe o' Auchterless,
There's manys a bonnie lass in the Garioch,
There's many a bonnie Jean in the streets o' Aiberdeen,
But the floor o' them a' is in Fyvie-o.

Like many old folk songs, the authorship is unattributed and is often cited as traditional. There are many different versions of the lyrics and it is often referred to by its opening line, *There Once was a Troop o' Irish Dragoons* or just *The Irish Dragoons*. The song is known by a variety of other names, the most common of them being *Peggy-o*, *Bonnie Barbara-o*, *Fennario* and *The Maid of Fife*. Not satisfied with travel to Fife, Pretty Peggy crops up in *Derby-o* and the song also appears in the American Civil War following the transit of Scottish immigrants. The song was popular in the Appalachians and a Dixie version of the song makes the final resting place of the captain to be Louisiana.

The earliest known version to be recorded was by the bothy ballad singer John Strachan in 1951. Bob Dylan is known to have recorded a version of *The Bonnie Lass* in 1962 then brought it back into his live set in the 1990s.

Bonnie Dundee

This spritely march is a very memorable tune with a 6/8 time signature (compound time) that provides a very definite rhythm which has the habit of getting kilts swinging whilst marching. In strict bass drum parlance, the beatings are one, two, three then pause, one, two, three then pause. The 6/8s are used as steady marches for drum major competitions or, in the context of pipe bands, as celebrations following a competition win, for example.

The words of the now famous folk song were written by Sir Walter Scott (1771-1832) but there is an older version of the lyrics with a title of *Jockey's Escape to Dundee*. The tune may have been composed by Charlotte Sainton-Dolby in the nineteenth century.

It was John Graham of Claverhouse (1648-89), 1st Viscount of Dundee, who was known as Bonnie Dundee. In 1689, after the overthrow of King James VII of Scotland (and II of England) by William of Orange, John Graham became a fervent supporter of the Stuart cause. Viscount Dundee had gained much experience fighting for the French King (Louis XIV) in a Scots regiment and he raised the standard on Dundee Law on 13th April 1689 in support of the Jacobite cause.

*Bonnie Dundee's
Breastplate*

Tae the Lords o' convention 'twas Claverhouse spoke,
E'er the King's Crown go down there are crowns to be broke,
So each cavalier who loves honour and me,
Let him follow the bonnets o' Bonnie Dundee.

Come fill up my cup, come fill up my can,
Come saddle my horses and call out my men,
Unhook the West Port and let us gang free,
For it's up with the bonnets o' Bonnie Dundee.

John Graham was also called Bluidy Clavers (Bloody Claverhouse) by his opponents, reputedly for the zealous manner in which he opposed the Covenanters and their conventicles in the south-west of Scotland. His greatest victory was at the Battle of Killiecrankie against a much larger Williamite force led by General Hugh Mackay. Using the steep ground to their advantage, the Highlanders were completely victorious but their leader, in the act of encouraging his men, was pierced beneath the breastplate by a musket ball, and fell from his horse, dying. Once propped up against a stone on the field by his comrades (now known as the Stone of Claverhouse) Graham reputedly asked a soldier:

"How goes the day?"
The man replied, "Well for King James,
but I am sorry for your lordship."
The dying, yet selfless, Graham replied,
"If it goes well for him, it matters the less for me."

The battle, although disastrous for the Government forces, was in reality the beginning of the end of the insurrection. The controlling and commanding genius of the rebellion that was Bonnie Dundee had perished. Unfortunately for the Jacobites, Killiecrankie had little overall effect on the eventual outcome of the war. Some historians believe that John Graham's charisma had a long-lasting impact in Scotland and inspired all of the future Jacobite risings. Quite a legacy for the man who was to become known as Bonnie Dundee!

The tune is very well liked and has been used as a regimental march by cavalry regiments in the main, including the Royal Horse Artillery of the British Army, several Canadian regiments and was also adapted by Confederate troops in the American Civil War. Another tune about the romantic figure of John Graham of Claverhouse is the pibroch, *The Lament for the Viscount of Dundee.*

The Braes o' Killiecrankie

This two-part 4/4 march is a rousing tune about the Battle of Killiecrankie. The first three verses and chorus were written by Robert Burns in 1789, exactly one hundred years after the battle was fought, to an older melody that was written not long after the battle. More recently, the song has been recorded by artists such as The Corries, Jean Redpath, The McCalmans and even Big Country!

The first Jacobite Rebellion, following the overthrow of King James VII of Scotland in The Glorious Revolution, is a particularly rich period of history for pipe tune inspiration.

Whaur hae ye been sae braw, lad?
Whaur hae ye been sae brankie-o?
Whaur hae ye been sae braw, lad?
Come ye by Killiecrankie-o?

An' if ye had been whaur I hae been,
Ye wadna been sae cantie-o,
An' if ye had seen what I hae seen,
On the braes o' Killiecrankie-o.

The Braes o' Killiecrankie refer to the steep-sided slopes on the banks of the River Garry just north of Pitlochry in Perthshire. This gorge was the dramatic setting for one of the key battles of the failed rising of 1689/90 (also called the Battle of Rinrory by contemporaries). The Jacobites, led valiantly by John Graham of Claverhouse (Bonnie Dundee), were pitched against a much greater Williamite force led by General Hugh Mackay on 27th July 1689. Using the steep ground to their advantage, the Highlanders fired a single volley at fifty metres, dropped their muskets and using axes and swords crashed into Mackay's centre which was swept away by the furious onset of Clan Cameron. John Graham, commander of the Jacobite army, was killed at the end of the battle, just as his forces were carrying the day.

During the battle, as the Jacobites pressed home their advantage, one of Mackay's soldiers, Donald MacBean, is said to have jumped across a river to safety. The feat is all the more impressive when we realise that the jump was 18 feet across the River Garry at what is now known as the Soldier's Leap. In making his leap, MacBean kept his life, but lost a shoe!

The Braes o' Killiecrankie was the last location that the two-handed broadsword (or claymore) was said to have been used to great effect.

Mackay blamed his defeat at Killiecrankie on the failure of his troops to fit the plug bayonet in time to stop the rush of the Highlanders and suggested it be replaced with the ring or socket bayonet.

A Claymore

Colonel Alexander Cannon of Galloway took control of the Jacobite army following the death of Bonnie Dundee, but had none of his tactical abilities nor charisma. Sir Ewen Cameron of Lochiel considered him a poor choice of leader, handicapped by his unfamiliarity with highland customs and inability to speak Gaelic.

Defeat came for the Jacobites at the Battle of Dunkeld on 21st August 1689, less than one month after their victory at Killiecrankie.

The Jacobites outnumbered the Government forces by four to one, but their tactics proved ineffective because the highland charge could not be deployed in the streets of Dunkeld.

The Cameronian Regiment was the mainstay of the Government force at Dunkeld. It was named after the Reverend Richard Cameron and was raised near Douglas by James, Earl of Angus, and placed into the service of William II of Scotland and III of England in April 1689. William Cleland masterfully conducted the defence of Dunkeld with raw troops. He had been appointed Lieutenant-Colonel having fought well at Drumclog and the Battle of Bothwell Bridge, but he was killed in action at Dunkeld aged twenty-eight and his body lies buried in the nave of Dunkeld Cathedral.

Following their defeat, the Jacobites were in poor spirit and many chose to return to their homes. James VII was occupied with preparations for resisting a threatened invasion of Ireland, and against this wider strategic backdrop only limited resources could be made available in Scotland, with James sending only clothing, arms, ammunition and provisions. James did send the Irishman Major-General Thomas Buchan, and at a subsequent council of war in Lochaber he was made commander-in-chief of the Jacobite forces in Scotland.

Major-General Buchan advanced his remaining men north through Badenoch, intending to march down Speyside and into the Duke of Gordon's country to seek much needed new recruits. Buchan reached Coulnakyle (near Nethy Bridge) on 29th April 1690, and ignoring counsel from his highland officers "not to advance past Coulnakyle", he continued the next day, but was intercepted at Cromdale, north-east of Grantown on Spey, by Sir Thomas Livingstone and his Government force…..

The Haughs o' Cromdale

This four part 2/4 march is popular with pipe bands and commemorates a battle that took place on Speyside in 1690. The battle occurred less than one year after Bonnie Dundee's victory at Killiecrankie. However, due to a mix of desertion and a need to tend crops, Major-General Buchan's rebel force had dwindled to only eight hundred men, comprising of the MacDonalds, MacLeans, Camerons, MacPhersons, the Invermoriston Grants and some Irish Jacobites. The remnants of this Jacobite army in Scotland were finally defeated on the Haughs of Cromdale between 30th April and 1st May 1690. A combination of surprise, the use of Government dragoons and poor Jacobite leadership on the field by Colonel Cannon were the likely deciding factors.

The Laird of Grant, a strong supporter of William, was much displeased that rebel soldiers were being quartered in plain sight of Castle Grant, harassing his lands, and so he sent for Sir Thomas Livingstone, Commander of the Government Garrison of Inverness. Livingstone arrived at Castle Grant, and although the Government troops could have rested, the eight hundred Grants among them were eager to march on and attack their foe at first light. So, the Government forces were on the move early, under the cover of darkness, and this element of surprise was to prove decisive.

Following some ingenious diversionary tactics in the river valley, Livingstone's cavalry crossed the River Spey and even though the Cromdale Kirk bells were sounded to warn the Jacobites, Livingstone was already in the ascendancy. He intercepted the unprepared Jacobites, who made only a brief stand at Lethendry at the foot of the Hills o' Cromdale where a small force, comprising Thomas Buchan, his nephew and the MacLeans, stood fast. It is this low ground, on the flanks of the Cromdale Hills, that entered into the tune name as The Haughs.

As I come in by Auchindoun,
Just a wee bit frae the toun,
To the Hi'lands I was bound
To view the Haughs of Cromdale.

I met a man in tartan trews,
Spiered at him (asked) what was the news,
Quo' he, "The Hi'land army rues
That e'er we come to Cromdale."

The Piper's Stone (Clach nam Piobair) above Cromdale is a little-known location, but one of some historical importance. During the battle, as the Jacobite force began to falter, athough badly wounded, a piper, frustrated by the ineptitude of his leaders, managed to drag himself atop this boulder and tried to rally his comrades by continuing to play tune after tune, motivating his men until he finally fell. The Piper's Stone now commemorates the death of the brave musician, but hillwalkers should beware for it is said that he returns sometimes during misty days, when he appears beside the unsuspecting visitor!

Livingstone's force used grenades to good effect, but fortunately for the outnumbered Jacobites a thick fog came down the side of the hill and enveloped them, compelling Livingstone to discontinue the engagement and not take up pursuit later in the day. A highlander, who was known as Tremearbag, was one of those who fell during the action and in the aftermath his Spanish gun, with long barrel and curiously carved fluted stock, came into the possession of the Stewarts of Glenmore.

The Jacobites, retreating from Cromdale after the loss of half their number, were mostly chased into Aberdeenshire by Mackay, but other small bands made a couple of attempts to regroup. A fleeing unit of around one hundred men (likely the Camerons and Macleans), who had separated from the main Jacobite force, crossed the Spey at Dallachapple. After being pursued by some of Livingstone's dragoons, they were overtaken and some were cut down on the moor of Grainish, just north of Aviemore, before they could take cover and refuge on the high ground of Craigellachie. Later, the remaining Jacobite stragglers, led by MacDonald of Keppoch, attempted to besiege the castle of Loch an Eilean in Rothiemurchus on the eastern side of the Spey, but their attack was repelled. It is believed that the castle was occupied mainly by the women, children and old folk of Rothiemurchus. One account of the attack had the 5th Laird of Rothiemurchus's resourceful wife, Grizel Mor (Big Grace), casting lead musket balls for the defenders and shouting abuse at the enemy.

Jacobean Pistol

Loch an Eilean Castle also played a role in later Jacobite uprisings, although with Jacobite sympathies more to the fore than in 1690. It was used in 1715 to confine Mackintosh of Balnespick in order to prevent him opposing the Jacobites, and after the Battle of Culloden in 1746, Jacobite fugitives were sheltered in the castle.

The action at Loch an Eilean, in May 1690, brought to an end the first attempt to restore James VII through force of arms within Scotland. One month later, General Hugh Mackay had returned his attention to the construction of Fort William, laying a cornerstone for the future pacification of the Highlands. The Stuart cause was dealt another blow two months after Cromdale with the defeat of James VII's forces by William of Orange at the Battle of the Boyne in Ireland in July 1690. The last vestiges of Jacobite resistance suffered their final defeat in July 1691 at Aughrim. The Battle of Aughrim in County Galway, western Ireland, was the bloodiest ever fought on Irish soil with over seven thousand killed between the two forces. It would be twenty-four years before Jacobitism would rise again.

The tune was originally written by James Hogg, the Ettrick Shepherd, but it had verses added to it anonymously that changed the essence of the song from a Jacobite defeat into victory by including an earlier battle at Auldearn in 1645. This earlier battle resulted in a victory for the Marquis of Montrose against a much larger Covenanter force.

> And the loyal Stewarts, wi' Montrose,
> So boldly set upon their foes,
> Laid them low wi' Hi'land blows.
> Laid them low on Cromdale.

> Of twenty-thousand Cromwell's men,
> A thousand fled to Aberdeen,
> The rest of them lie on the plain,
> There on the Haughs of Cromdale.

This amalgamation of two separate historical events, separated by forty-five years, but sung in reverse order, has resulted in a rather schizophrenic song which starts with a looming Jacobite defeat but the next day ends in victory. Although this pro-Jacobite composition has been economical with the historical facts - and artistic licence has been used to merge and describe the events out of sequence - it has made for a very popular song that appears to have stood the test of time!

Macpherson's Rant

This tune is a jaunty 4/4 march. Macpherson was a fine fiddler, and whilst in jail under sentence of death, he composed the tune *MacPherson's Rant*. Robert Burns rewrote the song, and called it *MacPherson's Farewell*, which no doubt helped to secure the tune for future generations. The tune is still very popular amongst Scottish fiddlers and pipers, underlining the power of song to transcend the centuries. It is doubtful that the story of James MacPherson would be known today without the legacy of his song.

MacPherson was an outlaw in the Highlands of Scotland and is said by some to be the Scottish Robin Hood. He was the illegitimate son of a highland laird, MacPherson of Invereshie, which is near Kincraig in Badenoch, Inverness-shire. His mother was a beautiful tinker girl that the laird met at a wedding. The laird acknowledged the child, once born in 1675, and had him reared in his house. After the death of his father however, the boy was reclaimed by his mother and Jamie became one of the travelling people, where he grew up "in beauty, strength and stature rarely equalled". He could handle a sword as expertly as he could a fiddle and eventually became a legitimate horse dealer and the leader of a band of gypsies. Although he was known to have been generous and popular with the poor people, he was the enemy of Lord Alexander Duff, the Laird of Braco. It was still, at that time, a criminal offence to be an Egyptian (Gypsy) in Scotland, so when Jamie MacPherson was first captured he was taken and held in jail in Aberdeen. However, his standing amongst the ordinary folk was such that an escape plan was hatched. His cousin, Donald MacPherson, and a gypsy named Peter Brown, heavily aided by local Aberdeen folk, broke into the prison, distracted and disarmed the guards and Jamie fled to cheering crowds.

Eventually, MacPherson was re-captured in Keith during the Saint Rufus Market Fair in September 1790. There are various versions of the capture but the story I prefer is that no-one would arrest him because he was such a fine swordsman. However, as he came into Keith with his piper leading him and his friends in gallus fashion, he became embroiled in a prearranged fracas. One of Jamie's party was killed and while trying to escape, a woman sitting at a window overlooking the narrow street threw down a thick heavy blanket which entangled him so he could not draw his sword. Jamie's sword was particularly unwieldy and the traditional belief that MacPherson was a big man is certainly justified by the length and weight of his weapon (it is preserved in Duff House, at Banff).

Jamie was tried in Banff on 8th November 1700 under the criminal statute of being an Egyptian (Gypsy). The court jury was packed with the dependants of Lord Duff, and Sheriff Nicholas Dunbar, allegedly a close friend of Duff, found him guilty. However, MacPherson enjoyed the protection of the Laird of Grant, and so a friend rode to the higher court in Aberdeen for a pardon, which was granted. MacPherson was to be hanged between the hours of two and three in the afternoon but when the Laird of Braco in Banff heard about a lone rider racing back via Turriff with the pardon, he ordered the town clock to be put forward by fifteen minutes so they could legally hang MacPherson just before the pardon arrived. Jamie was hanged at the Cross of Banff on Friday 16th November 1700, aged twenty-five.

Before the noose was tightened, MacPherson played his newly composed rant under the gallows, and then while in the noose he offered to give his fiddle to anyone who would play the tune at his wake. No-one took the instrument off the condemned man, so he smashed the fiddle over his knee, stating "No one else shall play Jamie MacPherson's fiddle". Traditional views in the north-east are that Jamie was using his tinker guile to entertain and occupy the crowd in an attempt to stall for time, but the pardon arrived too late to save his life - by the clock at Banff Cross at least!

Farewell ye dungeons dark and strang,
Farewell, farewell tae thee,
MacPherson's time will no be lang,
On yonder gallow's tree.

It was by a woman's treacherous hand,
That I was condemned to dee,
She stood uben a windae ledge,
and a blanket threw o'er me.

Sae rantingly, sae wantonly,
And sae dauntingly gaed he,
He played a tune and he danced around,
Below the gallow's tree.

A visit to the Clan MacPherson Museum in Newtonmore is well worthwhile as it will show you the broken pieces of Jamie's fiddle. The Banff Town clock was later relocated to Dufftown where it is known as "The clock that hanged MacPherson".

Even to this day, the nearby town of Macduff, just across the River Deveron, has its west-facing town clock covered so the people of Banff can't see the correct time and folks in the north-east still make jokes about the accuracy of the time in Banff!

Ye Jacobites by Name

Ye Jacobites by Name is a well-known and popular 4/4 march. The tune was written by the Scottish poet Hector Macneill (1746-1818) under the name *My Luve's in Germanie*. Robert Burns used the tune and rewrote it as *Ye Jacobites by Name* around 1791 and this is the version that most people know today.

The tune is an atmospheric traditional Scottish folk song which relates to the Jacobite risings in Scotland (1688–1746). The series of Jacobite risings are together called the Wars of the British Succession. The uprisings had the goal of restoring the Stuart line of kings to the throne (starting with James VII of Scotland, who was James II of England and Ireland). The 1715 and 1745 rebellions are the best-known attempts and just as Glenfinnan and Lochaber were important at the beginning of the '45 then Braemar and Aberdeenshire were at the centre of the '15 Rebellion.

John Erskine, the Earl of Mar, was born in Alloa, Clackmannanshire, in 1675, and in 1715 he placed himself at the head of the Jacobite cause. During August 1715 he met many of the highland chieftains at Aboyne, and with a favourable outcome they proceeded to hold their first council of war in Braemar on 27th August. It was here, on 6th September 1715, that the Earl of Mar proclaimed James VIII the King of Scotland, England, Ireland and France. The standard was raised at Castleton in Braemar, on the east bank of the River Cluny (near the Invercauld Arms) in the presence of six hundred supporters, and so began the Jacobite rising of 1715. The early part of the campaign in the north of Scotland was a success, the Jacobites taking Inverness, Aberdeen and Dundee within a month, and gradually the force under Mar's command grew to nearly twenty thousand men at its height.

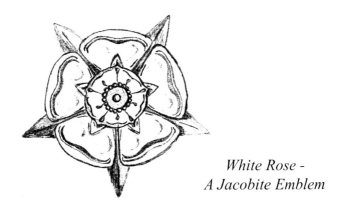

*White Rose -
A Jacobite Emblem*

Although his army grew in strength and number, as a general and military tactician, the Earl of Mar was an abject failure. Precious time was wasted at Perth, a feigned attack on Stirling was without result, and all the time Hanoverian forces were being reinforced by troops from Glasgow, Falkirk and Kilsyth.

The Earl of Mar finally left Perth and marched to Kinbuck by way of Auchterarder, where he was joined by General Alexander Gordon of Auchintoul and two and a half thousand highlanders. As the Jacobites marched south, the Duke of Argyll was marching his force north from Stirling towards Dunblane. By this time, Mar's forces outnumbered those of his opponent, John Campbell, the 2nd Duke of Argyll, by twelve thousand to four thousand, but importantly, the Government lines had many more cavalry.

Sheriffmuir was arguably the most important engagement of the '15 rebellion. The battle was fought on 13th November and was actually a draw as each army's right wing defeated the other's left wing in the military equivalent of a Viennese turn. General Alexander Gordon was the Jacobite military leader that made the most gains, leading a fierce highland charge that was said to have scattered the Government's left flank in only seven or eight minutes.

However, Mar's indecisiveness to press home this advantage, later in the day, with a force three times larger than the Government's, meant that in the aftermath the battle was to be viewed strategically as a decisive defeat for the Jacobites.

John Gordon of Glenbuchat, angry at Mar's lack of spirit, was said to have exclaimed to a battalion of Gordons from Auchintoul -

"Oh for an hour of Dundee."

- in reference to Bonnie Dundee's leadership and charisma. John Gordon had fought at Killiecrankie with Bonnie Dundee in 1689 as a boy of sixteen, was a man of forty-two at Sheriffmuir and was also present at the Clifton skirmish in 1745 and Culloden in 1746 at age seventy-two. Even as an old man, Glenbuchat had a formidable reputation amongst Hanoverians. He supposedly gave King George nightmares, and during the Jacobite march to Derby in 1745, King George is said to have exclaimed in alarm:

"De great Glenboggit is coming!"

On the same day as the Battle of Sheriffmuir, Inverness surrendered to Hanoverian forces led by the Earl of Sutherland, and a smaller Jacobite force was defeated at Preston. Mar retreated from Sheriffmuir to Perth. The fortunes of the 1715 rising had turned in a single day.

Mar was nicknamed Bobbing John for his tendency to shift back and forth from faction to faction, whether from Tory to Whig or Hanoverian to Jacobite. It may well have been this character trait of indecisiveness that made Bobbing John a poor military leader. Brigadier William Mackintosh, Laird of Borlum (1658-1743), was probably the best Jacobite military mind of the time and some believe that if he had been present on the open field of Sheriffmuir, instead of confined to the narrow streets of Preston, then the outcome of the '15 may have been very different. Following Preston, William Mackintosh was charged with treason, but he escaped from Newgate Prison with seven others the night before his trial was due to start. He escaped to France, but was to return four years later in 1719, this time with Spanish assistance, to catalyse another Jacobite rising.

The Pretender (James Francis Edward Stuart) belatedly landed in Scotland from France at Peterhead on 22nd of December 1715, and by the time he got to Perth in January 1716 the Jacobite army numbered less than five thousand men. The Jacobites retreated through Dundee to Montrose and Mar and the Pretender later discussed plans at Fetteresso, west of Stonehaven – but the cause was lost. Mar's revolt was over and on 4th February the Pretender wrote a farewell letter to Scotland. John Erskine and James Stuart fled in a boat from Montrose to France, where they both would spend the remainder of their lives. What was left of the Jacobite army of the '15 retreated to Aberdeen, then on to Badenoch, where it dispersed.

Ye Jacobites by name, lend an ear, lend an ear,
Ye Jacobites by name, lend an ear,
Ye Jacobites by name,
Your faults I will proclaim,
Your doctrines I maun blame, you will hear, you will hear,
Your doctrines I maun blame, you will hear.

An earlier version of the song simply attacked the Jacobites from a Whig point of view, warning the Jacobites not to take up arms, but Burns manages to communicate a deeper understanding of the internal struggle in the decision to take up arms or not, and in doing so brings a humanist anti-war outlook to the tune. In one of the verses the words have aspects of a protest song and Burns reinforces the sentiment of live and let live.

The Earl of Derwentwater's Lament

The Earl of Derwentwater's Lament is one of the most sorrowful slow airs ever written. It is also known as *Derwentwater's Farewell* but was previously known as *My Dear and Only Love Take Heed* from 1659 when it was published by John Gamble of Roslin. Lyrics may have been added later by Robert Surtees of Mainsforth in County Durham. Surtees is thought to have passed the tune onto James Hogg for later publication in The Jacobite Relics of Scotland which was originally commissioned by the Highland Society of London in 1817.

During the 1715 rebellion the northern English Jacobites were led by Sir James Radclyffe, 3rd Earl of Derwentwater (1689-1716), who had spent part of his youth as the companion of the young James VIII at Saint-Germain-en-Laye and so was a staunch Jacobite. He was an English Catholic nobleman, based at Dilston Hall, near Corbridge, and was extremely popular locally in the north of England.

Radclyffe joined with a force of Scottish borderer Jacobites led by William Gordon, 6th Viscount Kenmure. It was the Earl of Mar himself that appointed Kenmure, despite his total lack of military experience, commander of the Jacobite forces in the lowlands. Even though this small army was bolstered to four thousand at its height by a contingent of two thousand of Mackintosh of Borlum's men in Kelso, the sortie south of the border did not end well for this amalgam of Jacobite forces.

Mackintosh and his men had marched south from the Earl of Mar's main force, through Fife, crossing the Forth in fishing boats and capturing Leith. He daringly almost captured Edinburgh, then marched on to the border via Kelso, Jedburgh and Hawick. On crossing into England near Langholm, five hundred Mackintosh men were said to have headed for home, depleting the size of the force. The small army marched as far as Preston, where the Government forces caught up with them, leading to the Battle of Preston on 12-14th November 1715.

Sir Thomas Forster MP, despite having no prior military experience, was given overall command of the Jacobites at Preston. He immediately gave up a strong defensive position by retreating back into the town from Walton Bridge, which crossed the River Ribble immediately south of Preston. The Jacobites dug trenches and laid barricades and won the first day of the Battle of Preston, killing large numbers of the two and half thousand strong Government force. In a strange reversal of the history of the Battle of Dunkeld, 1689, it was the Hanoverian Cameronian Regiment that took the most losses against the Highlanders that were on this occasion defending the narrow streets. The next day, Hanoverian reinforcements arrived from Newcastle and, after some overnight Jacobite desertions, they realised they were outnumbered and surrounded, and they eventually surrendered to Major-General Wills. Captured Jacobites, numbering 1,468, with 463 of them being English, were rounded up in Preston's main square and taken prisoner. The prisoners were confined in the church and fed on bread and water for a month, and eventually many of the Highlanders were transported to the West Indies as slaves.

At the Battle of Preston, James Radclyffe argued for fighting their way out rather than surrendering. Radclyffe sided with the Highlanders in this argument, but was over-ruled by Thomas Forster, who appears to have taken command again after a period of panic, and he brokered the surrender. This battle, known as the Preston Flight, was the last battle to be fought on English soil, although some argue that it was more of a siege than a pitched battle.

After the surrender, both James Radclyffe and William Gordon (Lord Kenmure) were executed in London. They were both beheaded on 24th February 1716, gallantly declaring devotion to their Roman Catholic religion and proclaiming their allegiance to James VIII. On the night of the beheading, the northern lights were said to be unusually brilliant, and have since been known in some parts as Lord Derwentwater's Lights.

The Earl of Derwentwater's Lament serves as a reminder that the Jacobite rebellions were far more complex than the simplistic and factually incorrect assumption that it was Scotland against England. There was a large religious and cultural dimension to the Jacobite rebellions. The northern English Jacobite influence would raise its head again in 1745.

The Scottish Thistle and the English Rose

James' brother, Charles, the putative 5th Earl, also took part in the '15 rising and was likewise condemned but escaped from prison and fled to the continent. He returned thirty years later to join in the '45 rising. He was again captured and the next year the original sentence from 1715 was carried out, the Radclyffe brothers thus both (eventually) dying for their cause.

Farewell to pleasant Dilston Hall,
My father's ancient seat.
A stranger now must call thee his,
Which gars my heart to greet.

Farewell each friendly, well-known face,
My heart has held so dear.
My tenants now must leave their lands,
Or hold their lives in fear.

The beauty of this melody as a Northumbrian lament is unmatched when played on small pipes and if readers have not heard it then I recommend Louis Killen's version on his Northumbrian Garland EP from 1962. Roy Williamson of The Corries also does justice to this melancholic lament.

The Clan MacRae Society Pipe Band

This tune is one of the great 2/4 competition marches. It is a solid marching tune in simple time with two beats in each bar, each of which have the value of a quarter note, or crochet.

The composition was written by one of the founders of the modern pipe band movement, William Fergusson (1885-1949), who was born in Arbroath and was the composer of many other classic 2/4 marches, such as *The Australian Ladies* and *The Atholl and Breadalbane Gathering*. After serving in the First World War, he became Pipe Major of the City of Glasgow Pipe Band. The now legendary Clan MacRae Society Pipe Band was named after Farquhar MacRae who had earlier established the City of Glasgow Pipe Band. The name was changed in memory of MacRae in the 1920s after his death in 1916. William Fergusson, the composer of this tune, became one of the first of the modern era's great prize-winning pipe majors, leading the Clan MacRae to World Pipe Band Championships in 1921, 1922, 1923 and 1925. The band also won the World Championships in 1932, 1933, 1934 and 1953 under different leadership.

Eilean Donan Castle is the ancestral home of Clan MacRae, and this tune is used to tell the story of the castle's demolition by the Royal Navy in 1719 during a less well-known Jacobite rising that ended just a few miles up the glen from the castle at Glen Shiel in Kintail. This attempt to raise the clans for King James VIII garnered Spanish support in the form of three hundred troops and plentiful arms. The Jacobite force in the '19 rebellion totalled just over one thousand men, and in addition to the three hundred Spaniards the force included four hundred MacKenzies and MacRaes, one hundred and fifty from Clan Cameron, around one hundred and fifty Atholl men under Lord

George Murray, Mackintosh of Borlum and his men and other small clan groups, including the MacKinnons and the MacGregors led by one Rob Roy MacGregor. The size of the force could have been larger, but many of the mercenaries that sailed from Spain never reached their intended ports in south-west England because of a storm that wrecked troopships with the loss of many lives.

Eilean Donan Castle

Since the Jacobite force had more arms and ammunition than men, the excess was stored at Eilean Donan Castle, guarded by a Scotsman, an Irishman, two Spanish officers and thirty-nine Spanish soldiers left behind from the main force. On 10th May 1719 three British Royal Navy ships entered Loch Duich and anchored near Eilean Donan. The lead ship was the fifty gun man-o-war named HMS Worcester together with the twenty-five gun frigates HMS Enterprise and HMS Flamborough. The navy first sent in a small boat with a flag of truce to negotiate surrender, but it was met with cannon-shot from the castle. The ships then proceeded to bombard the castle, which was outgunned by one hundred to two cannons. The next day the navy captured the garrison and blew up what was left of the castle using the Spanish gunpowder that had been left behind.

James Keith, the 10th (and last) Earl Marischal, and William Murray, the Marquis of Tullibardine, argued about what to do next and who was to take command. Tullibardine produced a commission from 1717 appointing him leader of Jacobite land forces and recommended retreat, which Keith effectively prevented by ordering the two frigates back to Spain. On the route east to try to capture Inverness the Jacobite force was met by Government troops, led by the proactive General Wightman, in a steep-sided valley called Glen Shiel. Tullibardine led the Jacobites and prepared a strong defensive position south of the Five Sisters of Kintail, with the Spanish in the centre and the Highlanders on the flanks behind a series of trenches and barricades.

Wightman's well-drilled force arrived from the east about 4pm on 10th June and began the attack an hour later by firing their mortars at the Jacobite flanking positions. This caused few casualties, but the Jacobites had not encountered mortars before. In the subsequent disarray, Wightman's dragoons dismounted and advanced up the hill to their lines, then used grenades to bomb them out of their positions. Lord George Murray (Tullibardine's younger brother) and William MacKenzie, the 5th Earl of Seaforth, were badly wounded in the fray.

The battle lasted until 9pm when, due to a combination of failing light and smoke from burning heather (caused by the mortars and grenades), the Jacobites began to retreat, back into the hills to the west, leaving the Spaniards to surrender. The mountainside in Glen

Shiel, on which the battle mostly took place, is called Sgurr na Ciste Duibhe. This peak has a subsidiary top which was named Sgurr nan Spainteach (The Peak of the Spaniards) in honour of the Spanish Jacobean forces from Galica who fought admirably in the battle under Colonel Don Nicolás de Castro Bolaño.

At this engagement, eleven hundred determined and well-drilled Government soldiers and four Coehorn mortars were successfully deployed on steep hilly ground which usually benefitted the traditional highland charge. The Munro Independent Company, ably led by George Munro of Culcairn, were given a special mention in dispatches, having acquitted themselves well and in doing so, proving how important it was that Government forces knew how to fight effectively against their own countrymen. In addition to the Munros, the MacKays of Sutherland also fought on the Government side.

Thus, the Little Rising of 1719 ended in defeat for the Jacobites in the spectacular surroundings of Glen Shiel. The uprising did however encourage the British Government to take definitive action to prevent further trouble in the Highlands. Five years later, in 1724, General George Wade was sent to Scotland with a commission to build roads and barracks to ensure the stability of North Britain. Over a period of twelve years Wade constructed over two hundred and forty miles of roads, including thirty bridges.

As for Rob Roy MacGregor, his later life, as a cattleman and trader, was dominated by a personal feud with the Duke of Montrose. There had been a previous pardon for all those who had taken part in the '15 rising, but The Indemnity Act of July 1717 specifically excluded the whole of the Clan Gregor, including Rob Roy. This was because, just like his father, Rob Roy was a staunch Jacobite, being present at Killiecrankie in 1689, aged only eighteen, and within a stone's throw of Sheriffmuir in 1715 and, as we have just seen, was active again at Glen Shiel in 1719. Rob Roy MacGregor (1671-1734) received a royal pardon in 1726 which allowed him to live out his final years in peace, eventually dying at his house at Inverlochlarig Beg, Balquhidder, aged sixty-three.

Eilean Donan lay in ruins for two hundred years until purchased by a Colonel Macrae-Gilstrap, a descendant of the last Macrae constables of the castle. He spent from 1912 until 1932 reconstructing the castle and building it into what can be seen today. Eilean Donan Castle is now one of Scotland's most popular visitor attractions and is believed to be the most photographed castle in Britain. Above the main door reads a Gaelic inscription which when translated reads -

"As long as there is a Macrae inside,
there will never be a Fraser outside."

- which refers to a bond of kinship between the two clans. This gesture was reciprocated by the Frasers at their clan seat of Beaufort Castle near Beauly.

It is 2/4 marches that form the initial pieces in the March, Strathspey and Reel (MSR) format of performance and *The Clan MacRae Society Pipe Band*, as a six-part 2/4 march, has been a popular choice to start MSRs over the years.

MacCrimmon's Lament

MacCrimmon's Lament is a pibroch, which can be defined as an extended composition, played at a slow tempo, centred on a repetitive theme or 'ground' that is then embellished with slightly varying finger movements.

Donald Ban MacCrimmon, who was commonly believed to be the best piper in Scotland in the mid-1700s, allegedly had the power of second sight. *MacCrimmon's Lament* is also known as *MacCrimmon Will Never Return* because it surrounds the prediction of his death. This tune was composed after Donald's death by his brother Malcolm (both sons of Pàdraig Òg). The MacCrimmons were the hereditary pipers for the MacLeods of Dunvegan on Skye who were supporters of the Hanoverian lineage and fought against the Jacobites in the '45 rebellion.

A skirmish called the Rout of Moy took place in February 1746, two months before the Battle of Culloden. Moy, south of Inverness, is the ancestral home of the Mackintosh Clan chiefs. After the long retreat from Derby, Prince Charles Edward Stuart was being entertained as a guest of Lady Anne Mackintosh at Moy Hall. He had arrived from the south earlier in the day with a small guard of only fifty men, some distance ahead of his retreating Highland army. At the same time, Lord Loudon, the commander of the Hanoverian forces in the north of Scotland, had mustered fifteen hundred troops from the Independent Companies in Inverness. John Campbell was the 4th Earl of Loudon and while in Inverness he received information from Grant of Dalrachney regarding the presence of Charles at Lady Mackintosh's house, and importantly that he was attended by only a small bodyguard. So, with MacCrimmon playing his pipes at the head of the MacLeod column, Loudon set off south from Inverness Garrison towards Moy Hall just before midnight on 16th February in an opportunistic bid to capture the Bonnie Prince, who by this time had a £30,000 price tag on his head.

Pitch darkness interspersed with thunder and lightning both slowed and unsettled the men on the twelve-mile march south from Inverness to Moy along General Wade's road. Unknown to the detachment, a young boy called Lachlan Mackintosh had overtaken them, under the cover of darkness, to alert Lady Anne and the Prince. The 15-year-old lad ran with the warning from Lady Mackintosh's mother, who lived in Inverness, and had been tipped off about the Hanoverian plan. Coming from Moybeg, Lachlan knew the ground between Inverness and Moy well and he hid behind stone dykes and navigated the valley of the Nairn quicker than the redcoats, overtaking the troops just in time to get Lady Anne out of bed and allow preparations to be made!

After some initial panic, Lady Anne set to the task of protecting the Prince by sending him south and round Loch Moy and she then immediately called for her blacksmith, Donald Fraser. Within a short time, watching and waiting near the road, three miles north-west of Moy, was an outer guard of just five men, ably led by the blacksmith of Moy. He had chosen a clever location whereby they could observe movement on the skyline to the north, even in the darkness. Nearby, peat stacks remained out on the moor and using these for cover in the imposing terrain between the spur of Ciste Creag an Eòin and Meall Mor, he hatched a cunning plan to harass, and perhaps, just perhaps, deceive the enemy.

As the first troops of the Hanoverian column approached in the darkness, led by MacLeod of MacLeod, they were surprised by sudden musket fire and loud war cries urging clansmen to battle. Not only were the five men of Moy shouting at the top of their voices, but ingeniously they shouted the war cries of the Mackintoshes, MacPhersons, Camerons and MacDonalds and barked orders for their Lords Lochiel and Keppoch to advance their men on the right and left. This clever tactic, added to the choice of ground, the shrewd timing of the use of their weapons and several different points of attack, was no doubt a threatening and confusing sight and sound in the continuing lightning storm. Convinced that the whole Highland army lay ahead, and an ambush underway, Lord Loudon's men turned in panic and fled back to Inverness.

The Government troops hurriedly carried off the mortally wounded body of Donald Ban MacCrimmon, who had fallen at the feet of Lord Louden at the hand of the blacksmith's first discharge. MacCrimmon's premonition of his imminent death had been realised:

"Cha till mi tuille" (I'll return no more)

Donald Ban died of his wounds in Inverness. An eerie story from this time is that it was said that MacCrimmon was seen in Inverness the day before the engagement and "the shade of death was on him".

The tale of the Rout of Moy highlights the resourcefulness of the Five Men of Moy and the bravery of young Lachlan Mackintosh. Donald Fraser - Captain of the Five - and the mastermind behind the deception, died at Corrybrough in June 1804 and lies buried in Moy Churchyard - his blacksmith's anvil is still preserved at Moy Hall.

Another pibroch linked to Donald Ban's death is *The Pretty Dirk*, composed by his father Pàdraig Òg. The dirk in question was owned by Donald Ban's father, but because Donald was the family member accompanying his chieftain to war against the Jacobites he was given the dirk to carry while in service. The dirk was dropped either when Donald Ban was shot or when, in the ensuing panic, his body was quickly removed from the field in the dark of night. It was later recovered by Donald Fraser.

A Highland Dirk

The tradition of hereditary pipers allied to important Highland families is well known and other examples include the MacArthurs who played for the MacDonalds of Sleat; the MacGregors for the Campbells of Glenlyon; the Cummings for the Grants of Strathspey and Badenoch; the MacKays for the MacKenzies of Gairloch and the Rankins for the MacLeans of Duart, but undoubtedly, the most famous of them all were the MacCrimmons. Both the MacCrimmons and the MacArthurs were known to have piping colleges, where apprenticeships would last up to seven years.

The Skye Boat Song

This is a Gaelic rowing song, often sung to children as a lullaby, in a slow rocking 6/8 time. When played at the right tempo, and with feeling, *The Skye Boat Song* makes a beautiful Scottish waltz.

This song refers to the flight of Bonnie Prince Charlie between various Hebridean islands after the Battle of Culloden, which was the last pitched battle fought on British soil. This landmark encounter effectively ended the Jacobite rising of 1745 and the greater Jacobite cause.

The rising took place through 1745, but the battle itself took place on 16th April 1746 and by this point the Jacobite army was tired, hungry and demoralised after their long march back north from Derby. As the army retreated north, it had split up and Highlanders began to desert, or at least seek rest back in the glens.

Despite sound advice from the experienced Lord George Murray to take to the hills, regroup, and fight on more favourable ground (where mountain slopes could assist the highland charge), Bonnie Prince Charlie chose Drumossie Moor near Inverness as the place to stand against the Government army of the Duke of Cumberland, who was King George II's son.

Following the battle, where two thousand Highlanders lost their lives, many of the remaining Jacobites headed south and south-west into the hills, many towards Corrybrough and eventually they made their way towards Kingussie. Roughly fifteen hundred men assembled at Ruthven Barracks and received orders from Charles Edward Stuart to the effect that all was lost and to "shift for himself as best he could".

After the disaster of Culloden, Charles was chased westwards through the western highlands for months by Hanoverian troops. To evade the redcoats, he was forced to take circuitous routes via Glen Cannich, Glen Affric, Glen Shiel, Ben Alder (Cluny's cage), Borrodale, Benbecula, Skye, Raasay, Skye again then back to the mainland.

> Speed bonnie boat like a bird on the wing,
> Onward the sailors cry.

> Carry the lad that's born to be King,
> Over the sea to Skye.

Sadly, the Prince visiting Raasay for two days to seek refuge with the MacLeods of Raasay, who had supported him, was to lead to serious retributions from his Hanoverian pursuers. In particular, Captain Caroline Frederick Scott was an Edinburgh soldier who had an apparently brutal streak and relished his own notoriety. During this horrid, revengeful phase of Highland history, these retributions were not confined to Raasay. One of the other most notorious Hanoverians was Colonel Edward Cornwallis from London, who led three hundred and twenty redcoats to plunder and burn Lochaber. He targeted Achnacarry House, the home of Donald Cameron (Gentle Lochiel), who reportedly looked on as his family home was razed to the ground.

Major James Lockhart was a Lanarkshire soldier who fired Glenmoriston and Strathglass. Colonel John Grant led two hundred redcoats through Strathspey and Badenoch, setting fire to the home of Ewen Cluny MacPherson, Chief of the MacPhersons. Captain John Fergusson from Aberdeenshire was infamous for his abuse of prisoners, as was his accomplice, Captain Duff, who committed atrocities on the Island of Canna. MacLeod of MacLeod (known as Norman the Wicked) and his senior captain, MacLeod of Talisker, were also responsible for several atrocities.

During his wanderings, whilst the redcoats raped, murdered, plundered, drove off livestock and destroyed crops in an attempt to suppress Highland life and culture, Charles was assisted, at great risk to themselves, by a number of supporters. These brave companions included: his boatman and pilot Donald Macleod of Galtrigill (near Dunvegan on Skye); his faithful guide Alexander Macdonald of Glenaladale and also the Prince's friend and protector Angus MacDonald of Borrodale near Arisaig. However, it was Flora MacDonald that wrote herself into this song, and into history, by accompanying the Prince on his journey to Skye from South Uist. Famously, Flora MacDonald disguised Charles as her Irish serving maid (Betty Burke) to hide his identity. The Prince made the famous crossing of the Minch with Flora MacDonald, Neil MacEachain from South Uist plus four boatmen and landed on the Waternish Peninsula of Skye.

The tune itself is traditional in origin and this Gaelic air was probably called *Cuchag nan Craobh* (*The Cuckoo in the Grove*) before it was collected by Miss Annie MacLeod (Lady Wilson) when she heard it sung by local rowers on a boat trip across Loch Coruisk in the Black Cuillin on Skye in the 1870s. The English words were written in 1884 by Sir Harold Boulton (1859-1935), using a Jacobite theme, and it was he who introduced the heroic figures of Bonny Prince Charlie and Flora MacDonald. The version of the lyrics sung for the TV show Outlander are not Boulton's lyrics but a version of those penned in Robert Louis Stevenson's poem from 1892:

> Sing me a song of a lad that is gone,
> Say, could that lad be I?
>
> Merry of soul he sailed on a day,
> Over the sea to Skye.

Songs evolve through time, and *The Skye Boat Song* is one such example where the iterative process of collection, embellishment, refinement and improvement of a traditional tune has made it more popular, thus preserving the song and the story, allowing it to be retold by future generations.

Bonnie Galloway

The melody of *Bonnie Galloway* was written by the famous fiddler Neil Gow (1727-1807) and words were later put to it by Lady Nairne (1766-1845). Lady Nairne, who was known as Carolina Oliphant, also wrote words to *The Rowan Tree. Bonnie Galloway* and *Rowan Tree* are often played by pipe bands in the same 4/4 march set. Somewhat confusingly, the words of *Bonnie Galloway* are often credited to George G.B. Sproat and the music to George F. Hornsby. In more modern times, Jean Redpath was famous for her delivery of *Bonnie Gallowa'*.

> Wha but lo'es the bonnie hills,
> Wha but lo'es the shinin' rills,
> Aye for thee my bosom fills,
> Bonnie Gallowa'.
>
> Land o' darkly rollin' Dee,
> Land o' silvery windin' Cree,
> Kissed by Solway's foamy sea,
> Bonnie Gallowa'.

This tuneful score is very close in melody to *Will Ye' No Come Back Again* and this was supposedly directly addressed to Bonnie Prince Charlie at the time of his departure to France after the failed Jacobite Rebellion of 1745/6. The Prince's Cairn marks the traditional spot on the shores of Loch nan Uamh in Lochaber from where he made his final departure from Scotland. He left on the French frigate L'Heureux on 19th September 1746, in stark contrast to the hope in which he had arrived just over a year earlier.

Charles Edward Stuart was born in 1720 and spent his early years in Rome. He was the grandson of the exiled Stuart King. As the son of the Old Pretender, Charles quickly became known as the Young Pretender. He was twenty-four years old when he sailed from Nantes in the sixteen gun French privateer Du Teillay. He came ashore on the Hebridean island of Eriskay with his seven companions, later called the Seven Men of Moidart, on 23rd July 1745 and raised his royal standard at Glenfinnan at 1pm on 19th August.

Gradually, after much persuasion and appeals to honour, valour and historical allegiances, he gathered a Highland army of between one thousand and fifteen hundred men. Clan Cameron were one of the first clans to offer support and they were the largest contingent present at Glenfinnan. The Jacobites commenced their march to London via Perth, where a crowd of twenty thousand locals congregated and the nickname Bonnie Prince Charlie was first uttered. From Perth, the army continued to Edinburgh, and had early military success at the Battle of Prestonpans against Johnny Cope who was commander-in-chief of Scottish troops from 1743. The five thousand strong Jacobite army proceeded buoyantly into England, through Carlisle as far as Derby, hoping a popular uprising would oust the Hanoverian usurper, George II, and restore Bonnie Prince Charlie's father as the rightful heir to the throne. With momentum on their side, and only one hundred and twenty miles to go to London (probably only 6-8 days' march), the decision was made to turn the army around from Derby and retreat, the Jacobites having to retrace their steps.

Charles' soldiers were known as Jacobites (from the Latin Jacobus for James) in reference to his father, James Francis Edward Stuart (the Old Pretender). Charles' grandfather, James II of England, Ireland and VII of Scotland, ruled the countries from 1685 to 1688. He was deposed when Parliament invited the Dutch Protestant William III and his wife Princess Mary (King James' eldest daughter), to replace King James in the Glorious Revolution of 1688.

With the Jacobite cause lost at Culloden in April 1746, Charles spent the remainder of his life on the continent. There is one brief exception – which was his secret visit to London in 1750. Bishop Robert Gordon, a staunch Jacobite, had a house in Theobald's Row in Holborn and this was one of Charles' safe-houses for the visit.

Pope Clement XIII had recognised the Old Pretender as King of England, Scotland and Ireland (James III and VIII), but he did not give Charles (the Young Pretender) the same recognition when Charles' father died in 1766. Bonnie Prince Charlie died in exile in Rome on 31 January 1788 aged sixty-seven.

The melodies of *Bonnie Gallowa* and *Will Ye No Come Back Again* are inextricably linked, possibly through the tune *Bonnie Charlie* which was an alternative name for *Will Ye No Come Back Again*. The tribute to the region of Galloway was given a slightly varying melody and new lyrics with a Jacobite spin by Lady Nairne. This new composition referred to the departure of Bonnie Prince Charlie from Scotland.

Bonnie Charlie's noo awa,
Safely o'er the friendly main,
Mony's a heart will break in twa,
Should he ne'er come back again.

And mony a traitor 'mang the isles,
Brak the band o' nature's law,
And mony a traitor wi' his wiles,
Sought to wear his life awa.

And will ye no' come back again?
Will ye no' come back again?
Better lo'ed ye canna be,
Will ye no' come back again?

Lord Lovat's Lament

This tune was written as a lament to commemorate the execution of Lord Lovat for his part in the 1745 Jacobite rebellion. However, many pipe bands now play it with quicker tempo as a 4/4 march.

Lord Lovat is the hereditary chief of the Clan Fraser. Simon Fraser, the 11th Lord Lovat, was born in 1667 and was a remarkable character. He was nicknamed 'The Fox' and was one of the great political rogues of eighteenth century Scottish history. In 1715 he had been a supporter of the House of Hanover but by 1745 he had changed his allegiance and supported the Stuart cause.

Lord Lovat was not present at Culloden, (he had tried to hedge his bets by sending his son) but nonetheless, the Hanoverians were still keen on vengeance for his Jacobite scheming and plotting. After the Jacobite cause was lost at Culloden, Lord Lovat took refuge in various hiding places on his own estates and eventually made it to the west coast to be hidden by Macdonald of Morar and await passage to France. However, he was captured on an island in Loch Morar in June 1746 and transported to London in stages due to his advanced age.

Lord Lovat was executed for treason on Tower Hill on 9th April 1747 aged eighty. Lovat saw many spectators arrive at Tower Hill, and an overcrowded timber stand collapse, leaving nine spectators dead, to Lovat's wry amusement. Among his last words was a line of Horace: "Dulce et decorum est pro patria mori" - "It is sweet and seemly to die for one's country." So, he died in his own eyes, a Scottish patriot.

Simon Fraser of Beaufort was the last person in Britain to be beheaded for treason, and the axe and block used for this grizzly task are still on display at the Tower of London. At the execution, the chief's piper (David Fraser, 1716-1812) wrote *Lord Lovat's Lament*. Lovat is said to have looked forward to his internment in the family vault at Wardlaw Mausoleum at Kirkhill near Beauly with all the pipers from John o' Groats to Edinburgh playing at his funeral. But the Government refused to release his corpse for burial in Scotland and there is still huge conjecture about the final resting place of the Old Fox's body.

Axe and Block

Lord Lovat's son, Thomas (12th Lord Lovat), was eventually allowed to buy back the family's forfeited estates as a reward for raising two regiments and other service for the Government. And so, in 1757/58, The Fraser Highlanders were one of the first new Highland regiments to be raised following the Battle of Culloden, which is a reminder of the fact that in only ten years there occurred (for some clansmen) a transformation from rebels to royalists.

The Fraser family was to maintain its strong military links. The Lovat Scouts was a Highland regiment formed in January 1900 for service in the Second Boer War by Simon Joseph Fraser, 14th Lord Lovat. Recruited initially from gamekeepers on highland estates, they were the first known military unit to wear a ghillie suit (a type of camouflage clothing) and in 1916 they formally became the British Army's first sniper unit. The recruitment of gamekeepers meant that the unit was uniquely well-prepared to act in the role of sharpshooters. The 14th Lord Lovat was also responsible for the strong links between the War Office and the Piobaireachd Society, of which he was president from 1907 until his death in 1933. This is yet another example of a link between the pipes and the military. The love of the pipes would continue in the Lovat family lineage.

Amazing Grace

This well-known tune is a slow air with a melancholy feel that has made it a popular choice to be played at funerals. Its slow tempo makes *Amazing Grace* a good first tune to learn on the chanter but, although the finger work is not complex, holding the notes for the correct length of time proves difficult for some early learners. The origin of the melody is unknown, but it's likely to have been a traditional Scottish lament, with versions called *Gallaher* and *St Mary* thought to be antecedents.

The words were written by John Newton (1725-1807) who was a ship's captain on a vessel that plied the slave trade. On the night of 21st March 1748, on a homeward voyage, a terrible storm battered his vessel so severely that he became frightened enough to call out to God for mercy, a moment that marked the beginning of his spiritual conversion. He recorded in his journal that God had addressed him through the storm and that grace had begun to work for him:

Amazing grace, how sweet the sound,
that saved a wretch like me.

I once was lost but now I'm found,
was blind but now I see.

A Pipe Chanter

Newton's full conversion was not immediate, and he continued in the slave trade; however, he saw to it that the slaves under his care were treated humanely. By 1755, after a serious illness, he gave up seafaring forever. He began studying theology and was ordained by the Church of England in 1764. In 1767 the poet William Cowper and he became friends, and Cowper helped Newton with his religious services. Their goal was to write a new hymn for each weekly prayer meeting. *Amazing Grace* was written to illustrate a sermon on New Year's Day of 1773 and was first published in 1779.

The tune then travelled to the USA from the UK, possibly guising under the title of *New Britain* and passed through Kentucky and Tennessee to Virginia and South Carolina. In 1835 William Walker from South Carolina merged Newton's hymn with the melody we now recognize. A folk ballad such as this would have been passed orally and the tune is often attributed to be an early American folk melody. This status was augmented by its popularity in the American Civil War, where many deaths and burials would have been commemorated to the sound of *Amazing Grace*. The song is often referred to as the Cherokee National Anthem, although it is likely to have entered this community as a song that slaves sang. The tune featured in a highly popular anti-slavery novel called Uncle Tom's Cabin and entered into the African American gospel tradition, often with a strong emphasis on the sentiment of redemption.

In 1972 the Royal Scots Dragoon Guards recorded an instrumental version arranged for the bagpipes. It hit number one in the UK Singles Charts, spending twenty-four weeks in total in the charts and selling seven million copies worldwide by 1977. Nowadays, the tune is arguably the world's most famous folk hymn and is estimated to be performed globally around ten million times per year – with a large proportion at funerals.

The Barren Rocks of Aden

This well-liked, jaunty 2/4 march is popular with pipe bands. The fingerwork required for this tune gives the novice player a great opportunity to master the movement called the birl. Executed by the pinkie, the birl quickly combines several grace notes on low A to provide a pleasing sound that helps to give the pipes a unique signature, adding character to the instrument.

The Barren Rocks (as it is commonly referred to) was originally an unnamed composition written by piper James Mauchline who served with the 78th Highlanders from 1836-45. The tune was written in 1843 when he was stationed in Aden and it may have been penned because he was delighted that his regiment was leaving the hot, dry port? Alexander Mackellar was Pipe Major of the 78th Highlanders from 1853-62. Both Mauchline and Mackellar were members of the unit called the Ross-shire Buffs, later to become the Seaforth Highlanders. Mackellar re-arranged and named the tune. It was claimed that Mauchline's original tune was "acknowledged to be much in need of improvement" and Mauchline is said to have agreed that Mackellar's setting of *The Barren Rocks* was superior to his original. The tune was first published in The Ross Collection of 1869. The popular Scottish singer, Andy Stewart, put lyrics to the tune in 1963.

Aden is a port city in Yemen on the south coast of the Arabian Peninsula. It rains less than once a year in Aden and the Old Town is inside the shell of an extinct volcano with a district called Crater! Although *The Barren Rocks* was written long ago, Aden came back into the consciousness of the British people in the late 1960s. In 1967 the Argyll and Sutherland Highlanders were led by Lieutenant-Colonel Colin Campbell Mitchell, famously known as Mad Mitch.

Mitchell was born in south-west London on 17th November 1925. He was a British Army officer for most of his career and later, a politician. He became famous by leading the action which culminated in the British reoccupation of Aden, which at that time was a British colony.

Aerial View of Aden
Illustrating the
Volcanic Crater

This well-known story begins in June 1967. The Crater district had been taken over by nationalist insurgents and British forces were repulsed with the loss of 22 lives. Mitchell was determined to reoccupy it, though he had been warned that 500 well-armed police mutineers and terrorists had taken up positions there and were prepared to fight.

On the night of 3rd July, he ordered Pipe Major Kenny Robson to sound the regimental charge, the strathspey called *Monymusk*. Mitchell was of the opinion that the sound of the pipes stirred the blood and reminded him of the heritage of Scotland and the regiment. He believed it to be the most thrilling sound in the world and best of all - it frightened the enemy to death!

A burst of machine gun fire rattled out from the edge of the town, but the pipe major played on undeterred while his comrades flung themselves to the ground. None of them knew how much resistance would be encountered but as it turned out, the only person to be shot dead that night was a Yemeni man who had been challenged by British troops and attempted to run away. By the end of the night it was clear to Mitchell that his determination to push on into the Crater area had utterly demoralised the enemy. Not one British soldier was lost in this operation and at dawn on 4th July the pipes and drums sounded again from a rooftop overlooking Crater.

The crusade in which Mitchell most desired success, and to which he brought all his flair for publicity, was the high-profile campaign to 'Save the Argylls' at the end of the 1960s. In 1970, the Argyll and Sutherland Highlanders, as the junior regiment of the Scottish Division, faced disbandment as part of a general downsizing of the army. A compromise was brokered under which a single regular company retained the title and colours of the regiment. The 'Balaklava Company' continued as an independent unit from 20th January 1971 until the unit was restored to full battalion size on 17th January 1972. In this cause, Mitchell fell short of complete victory as the Argyll and Sutherland Highlanders status as a full regiment in the Scottish Division was no more.

Mitchell went on to become the Conservative MP for West Aberdeenshire from 1970-74 but did not seek re-election. He was a brave, clear-headed, loyal and intensely patriotic man. He had a gift for publicity but was impatient of opposition or incompetence. This is apparent from the lucid and absorbing account of his experiences in his book, *Having Been a Soldier* (1969). He died in 1996, age seventy.

My first and strongest memory of seeing a pipe band was at Hampden Park before a Scottish international football game in the late 70s with my dad, where the tune I liked most was *The Barren Rocks of Aden.* Nowadays, *The Barren Rocks* is a favoured choice for the country dance, The Gay Gordons, which often starts ceilidhs.

The 79th's Farewell to Gibraltar

This tune was composed by Pipe Major John Macdonald of the 79th Cameron Highlanders. It was written in June 1848 when his regiment left Gibraltar for Canada and is still considered one of the finest, most uplifting, 2/4 marches ever written for the pipes.

For three years the 79th Cameron Highlanders had been part of the garrison stationed on the strategic (but small) Rock of Gibraltar. The regiment was delighted to get 'off the rock' and go somewhere else. Pipe Major Macdonald composed *The 79th's Farewell to Gibraltar* to mark the happy occasion and decided to teach it to his pipers on the long Atlantic crossing to Canada.

Having crossed the Atlantic Ocean without incident, the fog on the St. Lawrence seaway presented a serious hazard. The sea captain was greatly concerned about a possible collision and asked the pipe major to take the pipe band up on deck to play as a warning to other ships of their presence. Macdonald decided to have them play their new tune. So, it was by giving *The 79th's Farewell to Gibraltar* its first airing that the ship avoided collision, and it's said that the bass drones were in tune with the ship's maritime foghorn!

*Rope-tensioned
Snare Drum*

John Macdonald was from Tiree, and it is famously recounted that he heard Allan MacLean from Mull piping for MacLean of Hynish when he was eleven years old. He heard tunes named *The Blue Ribbon* and *The Bratach Bhàn* and when he returned home he took out a chanter and played the tunes from memory, having only heard them once! Following Gibraltar and Canada, Pipe Major John Macdonald fought in the Crimean War, where the 79th Cameron Highlanders won two battle honours at Alma and Sevastopol. He lived to age seventy-two, dying in 1893. His two most famous compositions are *The 79th's Farewell to Gibraltar* and *The Dornoch Links*.

The Cameron Highlanders were raised in 1793 and were the only clan-raised unit with their own tartan which was not based on the Government tartan (worn by the Black Watch). Other Highland regiments (the Gordons, the Seaforths, the HLI and the Argyle and Sutherland) all wore variants of the Government tartan with different coloured stripes added. However, the tartan worn by the Cameron Highlanders Regiment was the distinctive red coloured Clan Cameron after Sir Alan Cameron of Erracht. In 1873, the regiment was met by Queen Victoria and at her request adopted the prefix of the Queen's Own. Following the Defence Review, the Queen's Own Cameron Highlanders were merged with the Seaforth Highlanders in 1961 to form the Queen's Own Highlanders (Seaforths and Camerons) and later merged with the Gordon Highlanders to form the Highlanders (Seaforths, Camerons and Gordons).

The tune was written with four parts but often only the first two parts are played. The march was particularly effective if troops were required to move quickly to a new location or in more recent times, played as the opening march in March, Strathspey and Reel (MSR) compositions.

The Green Hills of Tyrol

The Green Hills of Tyrol is a 3/4 march and this time signature is classified as a retreat march. They were originally played to signal a troop manoeuvre in battle but are now played when soldiers return to their barracks or camp at the end of the day.

The tune was originally from the opera William Tell by Rossini (1829) and Tyrol refers to a part of western Austria in the foothills of the Alps. The melody was transcribed to the pipes in 1854 by Pipe Major John MacLeod after he heard it played by a Sardinian military band when serving in the Crimean War with his regiment, the 93rd Sutherland Highlanders.

On 25th October 1854, only the Sutherland Highlanders, under Sir Colin Campbell, stood between the Russians and the port at Balaklava, the capture of which would have ended the Crimean campaign there and then. Pipe Major MacLeod and five other pipers participated in the episode that made the regiment's reputation - The Thin Red Line.

As the Russian heavy cavalry rolled down the hill onto the 93rd, the five hundred Scots were told by Colin Campbell (1st Baron Clyde):

"There is no retreat from here, men.
You must die where you stand."

The 93rd stood its ground, in two ranks, firing controlled volleys into the attacking Russian cavalry squadrons. The cavalry faltered and veered to the left of the 93rd, exposing their flank to more fire. The repelling of a heavy cavalry charge by grossly outnumbered infantry was an unprecedented achievement and the feat immortalised the 93rd as The Thin Red Line. Thin was used in the description since volley fire was usually given in ranks of four rather than a firing line of only two.

Unfortunately, the debacle of the Charge of the Light Brigade, later that same day, led to a stalemate at Balaklava and the war dragged on throughout the winter of 1854/55. The Light Brigade was not completely destroyed, but did suffer terribly, with 118 men killed, 127 wounded and about 60 taken prisoner.

When the Crimean campaign finally ended, the 93rd were immediately dispatched to China but en-route were given new orders in Cape Town to take part in the fight to quell the Indian Mutiny. In the Indian campaign, MacLeod distinguished himself at the Siege of Lucknow when he was first through the breach, and quickly struck up his pipes to encourage others over the wall. He was complimented after the battle but humbly replied:

"I thought the boys would fight better
with the national music to cheer them on."

Pipe Major MacLeod was well liked in his regiment and had a reputation for selflessness and amiability.

The tune was brought into popular culture in the 1960s by Andy Stewart. He put words to it in 1961 and the song became better known to many as *A Scottish Soldier*. *The Green Hills of Tyrol* is undoubtedly the best known and most recognisable 3/4 march played by pipe bands today. It is often played as the first tune in a three-tune retreat set along with *The Battle's O'er* and *Lochanside*, and this has become a classic arrangement played by massed bands at many highland games. It is certainly here to stay!

The Old Rustic Bridge (by the Mill)

This tune makes a great 4/4 march. It is an Irish song and so its popularity with Scottish pipe bands is testament to the strong musical links that existed, and still exist, between the Celtic nations. The tune was composed by Thomas Peter Keenan (1866-1927) who was known in his professional life as Tommy Conway. He was a versatile and prolific song writer and his other compositions include *When Irish Eyes are Shining, Mother Macree* and *That's an Irish Lullaby.*

This very well-known melody refers to an old bridge in Castletownroche, County Cork, Ireland. The old stone bridge spans a strategic crossing point of the River Awbeg. Incorporated into the present structure are the remains of a medieval bridge shown on a map of 1641 which demonstrates the bridge's antiquity.

The Old Rustic Bridge

I'm thinking tonight,
Of the old rustic bridge,
That bends o'er the murmuring stream,
It was there Maggie dear,
With our hearts full of cheer,
We strayed 'neath the moon's gentle beam.

'Twas there I first met you,
The light in your eyes,
Awoke in my heart a sweet thrill,
Though now far away,
Still my thoughts fondly stray,
To the old rustic bridge by the mill.

Thomas Keenan dedicated *The Old Rustic Bridge by the Mill* to his wife, Margaret Lillis, whom he married in the early 1890s. A plaque commemorating T. P. Keenan, whose remains lie in the graveyard overlooking this site, can still be read close to the bridge.

The Heights of Dargai

This tuneful and swinging march is often played alongside *The Battle of the Somme* which shares this uncommon 9/8 time signature (compound time with three beats to the bar) and melodic scheme. The tune was composed by John Wallace of Edinburgh who is also known for composing, among others, *The Henderson March* and *The Circassian Circle*. However, perhaps his most famous tune is the hornpipe called the *CTS Empress*, which refers to the Clyde Training Ship, the Empress, which was moored off Rhu in the Gareloch and provided care for four hundred homeless boys. John Wallace took up employment as an instructor on the Empress in 1898/99 and within six months he had trained up and turned out the Empress Juvenile Pipeband which was apparently of good standard and was known to play often at the bandstand in Helensburgh.

The Heights of Dargai commemorates the bravery of the Gordon Highlanders Regiment at the battle in 1897 at the Heights of Dargai in northern India (modern day Pakistan) during the Tirah campaign. Somewhat confusingly, there appears to be another name for this composition, which is *The Dagshai Hills*, which may be the original name, even though Dagshai is 700 km east of Dargai.

In October 1897, the British Army tried to quell the rebellion of one of the main tribes called the Afridi. The Dargai Heights commanded the entrance to a pass that was of great strategic significance. The three hundred yard high cliffs of Dargai were a rocky outcrop that offered an excellent natural defence for the eight thousand Afridis.

Pressing west from Kohat, on 18th October, the British force, led by General Sir William Lockhart, passed through the Khanki

Valley and began to attack the cliffs of Dargai. Although some cliffs were taken, they could not be held due to the lack of water in the heights and also because of incessant stiff counter-attacks from the Afridis.

On 20th October the Dorset and Devon Regiment and the Ghurka Rifles attacked, again to no avail, and it was then that the Gordon Highlanders eventually received the order to join the fray. To the sound of the pipes, they climbed the cliffs under heavy fire from the Afridis. There were five pipers at the start of the action but only one made it to the top.

Famously, the junior piper, Findlater, was hit in both ankles by bullets, but even in excruciating pain he still managed to lean against a rock and continue to play his battle-damaged pipes until he passed out. He inspired the Gordons forward to a quick victory in only forty minutes. There is some conjecture as to the tune played by Findlater, but it is said that although *Cock of the North* was called for, Findlater chose *The Haughs o' Cromdale* to better inspire the men. He later shared his thinking, that *The Cock of the North* was more of a classic march and that *The Haughs*, as a strathspey, was more of what was required for a quick assault!

Findlater became disabled from the wounds he sustained in Dargai and was repatriated for treatment. He was awarded the Victoria Cross (the highest and most prestigious award in the British Army for heroism and courage) on 16th May 1898 by Queen Victoria herself for the bravery he displayed during the Battle of Dargai.

For background, George Frederick Findlater was born at Forgue, near Turriff in Aberdeenshire, in 1872. He joined the Gordon Highlanders in 1888 and served in Belfast, Ceylon and Chitral in

India. Following Dargai, Findlater was unfit for further service, but such was his celebrity status after his decoration he was able to command considerable fees by playing his pipes in popular music halls. By the time war broke out in 1914 George Findlater was a 42-year-old farmer, farming at Forglen near Turriff, but he re-enlisted for the 9th Battalion of The Gordon Highlanders. He travelled to France with the battalion in July 1915 as a sergeant piper and was wounded at the Battle of Loos. Invalided out of the army for the second time, he returned to his farm in Aberdeenshire and became the Pipe Major of the Turriff Pipe Band in the inter-war period. On 4th March 1942 George Findlater VC, the Piper of Dargai, died of a heart attack aged seventy years and is buried near Turriff.

Findlater's military decoration of the Victoria Cross is displayed at the Gordon Highlanders Museum on Viewfield Road, just off Queens Road in Aberdeen. This museum is housed in the former regimental headquarters of the Gordons and is recommended to anyone interested in the Gordon Highlanders – it's certainly worth a visit! Many famous paintings exist that commemorate this action including The Storming of the Heights of Dargai by Vereker Monteith Hamilton (1856-1931).

The Gordon Highlanders had been raised by Alexander, the 4th Duke of Gordon, in 1794 in response to the threat posed by the French Revolution and were originally known as the 100th Regiment of Foot (later renamed the 92nd in 1798). The early recruitment campaigns were assisted by Alexander's wife, the Duchess of Gordon (Duchess Jean), who is said to have offered a kiss to those that signed up. Many of the original recruits were from the Gordon estates and the regiment has been long associated with the North-east of Scotland. Under the Childers Reforms, it amalgamated with the 75th (Stirlingshire) Regiment of Foot to form the Gordon Highlanders in 1881.

Gordon Family Crest

The cap badge of the Gordon Highlanders Regiment bore the royal stag head of the Marquis of Huntly which sits on a Duke's crown, intertwined with ivy that also represents the Gordon family. Bydand was the motto of the Gordon Highlanders, which is an old Doric motto, shortened from the phrase 'Bide and Fecht' meaning 'Stay and Fight'. In more modern vernacular it's often translated to 'Steadfast' or 'Endure'. Famously, Winston Churchill stated in 1900 that the Gordon Highlanders "were the finest regiment in the world."

In 1994, exactly two hundred years after the formation of the original regiment, the Gordons were amalgamated with the Queen's Own Highlanders to form The Highlanders (Camerons, Seaforths and Gordons). In 2006, following further rationalisation, the Highlanders became the 4th Battalion of the Royal Regiment of Scotland (4 SCOTS). It is within this new identity that the legacy of the Gordon Highlanders lives on and continues to inspire - Bydand Forever!

The Battle's O'er

When the Battle is Over (to give the tune its full name) is a melodic and appropriately titled 3/4 retreat march which is in simple time and has three beats in the bar, each to the value of one crotchet or quarter note.

The tune is a late nineteenth century composition by Pipe Major William Robb (1863-1909) of the Argyll and Sutherland Highlanders, and the tune entered piping repertoires between the Boer and the First World Wars. Robb followed his father into the army and joined the same regiment as a red-haired lad, aged thirteen, where he was listed as a drummer. He would later be listed as a piper, studied under the great Pipe Major Robert Meldrum and was Pipe Major of the 2nd Battalion Argyll and Sutherland Highlanders from 1887-91, and of the 1st Battalion from 1891-94.

Six years before Robb became pipe major, The Argyll and Sutherland Highlanders Regiment was created under the Childers Reforms in 1881 by the amalgamation of the 91st (Argyllshire Highlanders) and 93rd (Sutherland Highlanders) Regiments. The new regiment wore a version of the Government Sett (Government No.2A) as its regimental tartan and was also well known for sporting the swinging six sporran and for having the largest cap badge in the British Army.

In addition to the timeless *The Battle's O'er*, Robb also composed the excellent 2/4 competition march *The 91st Argylls at Modder River*, and was also a very stylish player of strathspeys and reels. In his day, he was most well known for a test march he made with Pipe Major James MacKay, another Argyll and Sutherland Highlander, when in 1895 the two men marched 35 miles from Aldershot to Hyde Park Corner, playing alternately all the way.

Glengarry of the Royal Regiment of Scotland

The Battle's O'er march bears a strong resemblance to the melody *The Last Rose of Summer* by Thomas Moore (1779-1852), an Irish poet, singer and songwriter. Thomas Moore is considered Ireland's National Bard and is to Ireland what Robert Burns is to Scotland. He is now best remembered for the lyrics of *The Minstrel Boy*. Andy Stewart put words to *The Battle's O'er* in 1961 where he encourages soldiers to sleep in peace - sleep in peace, now the battle's over.

It's a song whose gentle melody and words can hopefully bring comfort to ex-service men and women in the years after their career in the armed forces. Help for Heroes is the UK's leading charity for the armed forces community. This charity supports those with injuries and illnesses that are attributable to their time in service and more information can be found at www.helpforheroes.org.uk

Lochanside

Lochanside is a 3/4 march but is distinctive from other 3/4s by its phrasing, considered by many as uniquely memorable and pleasing. Played solo or in pipe bands, the melody has rare qualities and is unusual in having three parts rather than two. It is perhaps most commonly played in the guise of a long march to end the massed bands retreat set that includes *The Green Hills of Tyrol* and *The Battle's O'er*, and it will no doubt continue to be ever-present in pipe band repertoires.

The tune was composed by Pipe Major John McLellan DCM who was born in Dunoon on 8th August 1875. Little is known about his early piping life, or even who taught him, and this was perhaps partly because he was known to be modest to a fault and would very rarely talk about himself. John McLellan enlisted in the Highland Light Infantry in 1892, age seventeen, and went with the 1st Battalion to Malta in 1897. It was at this point that he began naming his compositions after places where he had served or people that he had served with.

His Distinguished Conduct Medal (DCM) - which is the second-highest British military decoration after the Victoria Cross - was won for his courageous conduct during the Battle of Magersfontein in South Africa. This battle was a critical engagement in the Boer War and it took place on 11th December 1899 near Kimberley, north-east of the Modder River. Pipe Major McLellan rallied the troops to the sound of his pipes while he was seriously wounded in the ankle. In memory of this moment, he later wrote *Lochanside*.

The dawn assault on Magersfontein Hill went badly because the Highlanders progress was greatly slowed by barbed wire. Unable to move forward or backward, they fell to the ground behind whatever cover they could find. The sun came up, revealing the brigade pinned down in front of the Boer positions. Whenever a soldier moved he attracted fire so they had no option but to stay there for the rest of the day, tormented by a mix of snipers, hot sun, thirst and being overwhelmed by swarming ants while trapped by the barbed wire. Some say that this account of the battle explains why McLellan was compelled to pen *Lochanside* with its unique qualities; neither able to move forward, nor retreat, his melody seems somehow to express the soldiers' predicament.

The British casualties at Magersfontein were 902 versus 236 Boers and, together with Stormberg and Colenso, these three defeats made up the Black Week of the Boer War. The losses in the Highland Brigade were felt keenly at home, causing great distress back in Scotland.

After the Boer War, McLellan left military life and in 1903 he joined the Govan Police Pipe Band in Glasgow before returning to Dunoon around 1905. During the Great War (1914-18) he was a piper in the 8th Argyllshire Battalion of the Argyll and Sutherland Highlanders and served with the 51st Highland Division on the Western Front, where he was wounded in action at Laventie in France. He became Pipe Major of the 8th Argylls in 1919 and held that position until he retired in 1930. In later life he was active in the piping scene around Dunoon and left a strong legacy after helping the local Boys' Brigade band and teaching the Dunoon Grammar School Cadet Pipe Band.

Known to friends and family as Jock, McLellan was a quiet and shy man, but who composed some of the most enduring melodies in pipe music. Pipe Major John McLellan DCM died in 1949 at the age of seventy-three and was buried in Dunoon Cemetery with full military honours. His friends and the Dunoon Town Council got together and erected a memorial plaque in his honour, and it is situated in the Castle Gardens in Dunoon, opposite the pier.

In addition to *Lochanside*, which is arguably his most loved tune, McLellan's other contributions are *The Highland Brigade at Magersfontein, Heroes of Vittoria, The Bloody Fields of Flanders, The Dream Valley of Glendaruel, The Road to the Isles* and *The Cowal Gathering*. Intriguingly, many of his compositions were 3/4 retreat marches, and this period from the Boer War through to the end of the First World War appears to have been when the penning of 3/4 retreats was at its height. Most of his compositions were published in the Cowal Collection of Highland Bagpipe Music.

The lochan in question in the title of the song is actually Loch Loskin (often referred to as the Lochan), which can be found to the north-west of Dunoon's town centre, within walking distance of the Cowal games park.

Lyrics to *Lochanside* were written by Jim Malcolm, previously the singer in the Old Blind Dogs from 1999-2006.

The Battle of the Somme

The Battle of the Somme is a march with a rare 9/8 time signature that lends itself beautifully as accompaniment to a highland dance called the Scottish Lilt. Although other tunes for the lilt could be *Drops of Brandy* or *Brose and Butter*, it is almost mandatory to play *Battle of the Somme*, largely because of its idiosyncratic 9/8 timing, which suits the steps to perfection.

This march was written by the renowned pipe tune composer William Lawrie (1881-1916) and commemorates one of the largest and most terrible conflicts of the First World War. Lawrie fought in the horrendous Battle of the Somme, where he became ill as a result of trench conditions and died in England shortly after, but he lived just long enough to see his tune meet immediate success. His death at only age thirty-five remains one of piping's greatest losses of young life.

William Lawrie was born into a slate quarrying family in Ballachulish, Argyll, and was the son of Hugh Lawrie, who gave him his first lessons on the pipes. Later he was taught by John MacColl, with whom he remained friends throughout his brief life. In 1910 he became only the second piper ever to win the gold medals at both Oban and Inverness in the same year, and he added the clasp the following year. In 1914 he succeeded George Ross as Pipe Major of the 8th Battalion of the Argyll and Sutherland Highlanders and accompanied them to France in 1915.

The Battle of the Somme began when the whistles blew at 7.30am on 1st July 1916 and a colossal 57,450 casualties were sustained by the British troops on the very first day. Most of these fell in the first hour or so. The battle became a protracted affair lasting until 18th November 1916. During the 141 day engagement, more than three million men fought in the battle and one million men were wounded or killed, making it one of the bloodiest battles in all of human history, and four hundred and twenty thousand of them were from the British Army. Given the large loss of life, one can be forgiven for being surprised, upon first hearing this tune, by the somewhat jaunty, yet powerful, melody of *The Battle of the Somme*, which belies the horrors of the First World War.

The Scottish troop involvement in this battle was considerable. Three Scottish divisions took part (the 9th, 15th and 51st Highland Divisions) and in total fifty-one infantry battalions took part in the action at some time. Some Scottish battalions, such as the 16th Royal Scots (the famous McCrae's Battalion) who took part in the first day's attack, suffered badly. This battalion, like many others, were pals' battalions raised locally, and the 16th, which was raised in Edinburgh, included the whole of the Heart of Midlothian first team, which signed up en-masse. Almost three quarters of the battalion were killed or wounded on 1st July, including many of the Heart's line-up, and by the end of the war seven of the team would have made the ultimate sacrifice.

Pals' battalions were also called service battalions and from Glasgow came the 15th HLI who worked on the trams; the 16th HLI was known as the Boys' Brigade Battalion and the 17th HLI who were made up of men who had previously worked in the Glasgow Chamber of Commerce.

Bantam battalions were also raised, specifically for men who did not reach the 5'3" (160 cm) minimum height for a British soldier. The first of these units came from Birkenhead in Cheshire after a local MP had heard that a group of miners had been rejected by local recruiting offices.

Another inspirational story from this part of the Western Front during the First World War concerns piper Jimmy Richardson from Bellshill near Glasgow, who had moved to Vancouver and then joined up. James Cleland Richardson (1895-1916) was a posthumous recipient of the Victoria Cross. He was a piper in the 72nd Seaforth Highlanders of Canada, 16th (Canadian Scottish) Battalion, Canadian Expeditionary Force.

During the Battle of the Ancre Heights on 8th October 1916 at Regina Trench, Piper Richardson had been detailed to play the company over the top. Following the whistle, the men got bogged down around barbed wire and their commanding officer was killed. Bravely, Piper Richardson continued to stride up and down whilst playing his pipes. His playing so inspired the company that the wire was rushed and the German position captured.

As often occurred during battle, the piper was detailed to take back a wounded comrade and some prisoners and, because his hands were full, he laid his pipes down. Later he insisted on turning back to recover his pipes which he had left behind in no-man's land. He was lost in action. His body now lies in Adanac Military Cemetery, France.

Four pipers played at the head of the companies as the Canadians went over the top that day; pipers John Park and James Richardson did not return.

Richardson's bagpipes were believed to have been lost in the mud of the Somme. However, a British Army chaplain, Major Edward Yeld Bate, had found the pipes in 1917 and brought them back home after the war to a school in Scotland where he was a teacher. The pipes served as a broken, mud-caked and blood-stained reminder to the pupils of the sacrifice made by an unknown piper from the Great War. They were unidentified for nearly ninety years until 2002, when the Pipe Major of The Canadian Scottish Regiment (Princess Mary's) responded to an internet posting. He discovered that Ardvreck Preparatory School in Scotland was in possession of a set of bagpipes with the unique Lennox tartan on them, the same tartan used by the pipers of the 16th (Canadian Scottish) Battalion.

A huge collective effort led to conclusive evidence that the pipes were those played by Piper Richardson on that fateful day in 1916. In October 2006, a party of Canadian dignitaries visited Scotland to receive the pipes from the Headmaster of Ardvreck School in Crieff for repatriation to Canada. The pipes are normally on display in the entrance hall of the British Columbia State Legislature building on Vancouver Island.

The Bloody Fields of Flanders

This pipe tune is a 3/4 march and was written by Pipe Major John McLellan of Dunoon (1875-1949). However, *The Bloody Fields of Flanders* may have begun life as an old Perthshire song called *Busk Busk Bonnie Lassie* or *Bonnie Glenshee*. Although difficult to untangle the tune's origins, the melody was very clearly used as the vehicle for the 1960s folk song *Freedom Come all Ye* by Hamish Henderson.

McLellan wrote the tune to commemorate the huge loss of life on the Western Front in the First World War. Almost seven hundred thousand Scots served in the Great War (1914-1918), with one hundred and fifty thousand losing their lives. The Flanders region in Belgium is synonymous with the First World War because this area saw some of the fiercest fighting. Trench warfare took place here over a four-year period as men dug in at locations such as Passchendaele, Ypres and Lys. At Ypres alone, around one million men of both sides are known to have lost their lives.

The First World War is when the nickname Ladies from Hell was given by the Germans to the kilted regiments of the British Army. The alternative Devils in Skirts nickname was supposed to have been given to the soldiers of the 51st Highland Division during the Battle of Ancre in 1916, and the nickname hints at the fierce warrior spirit of the Scots. The sound of the pipes would have undoubtedly added to the uniqueness of the Scots at war, firstly because of the volume of the Great Highland Bagpipe and secondly, that the pipes are the only instrument in the world said to skirl!

The melody to *The Bloody Fields of Flanders* has had a lasting legacy. The well-known Scottish poet and songwriter, Hamish

Henderson (1919-2002), penned the words to *Freedom Come All Ye* in 1960 after he heard *The Bloody Fields of Flanders* played in 1944 on the Anzio beachhead in Italy in the Second World War. His words have an anti-imperialist sentiment, but cleverly this message is coupled with a subtle pride and recognition of the part that Scots played in the British Army. The role of the Scottish soldier is renounced in both its forms; cannon fodder for a larger empire-building entity and also as the colonial oppressor. Loss of life in the name of conquest and subjugation of other peoples is rejected and there is a strong sense of anticipation of the day when all peoples are truly free - *Freedom Come all Ye* - and can meet in peace and friendship.

First World War Military Cemetery
"We will remember them"

Henderson's words are broad Scots and have been evocatively delivered by Dick Gaughan over the years. Should you wish to listen to non-Scots versions of the song then Luke Kelly sang this in his broad Dublin accent, and Pete Seeger sang it in his American accent. A version of the song was performed by South African soprano Pumeza Matshikiza at the opening ceremony of the 2014 Commonwealth Games in Glasgow.

Henderson later described the song as "expressing my hopes for Scotland, and for the survival of humanity on this beleaguered planet". Some people believe that the tune has the winds of change qualities necessary to be a modern national anthem for Scotland, though Henderson himself felt that part of its strength comes from its wider reaching potential status as an international anthem. Who could argue with Henderson's wish to have the song represent the vision of world peace, given all the losses, of all nations, that made the fields of Flanders bloody?

Highland Laddie

Highland Laddie is a well-known 2/4 march whose melody is instantly recognisable. Pronounced *Hielan' Laddie* in Scots, the tune was adapted by Robert Burns from an old popular folk tune called *If thou'lt Play me Fair Play*, but is also reminiscent of *The Bonnie Lass of Livingston*, *Cockleshells* and *High Caul Cap*. Here are the words that Burns penned in 1796:

> The bonniest lad that e'er I saw,
> Bonnie laddie, Highland laddie,
> Wore a plaid and was fu' braw,
> Bonnie Highland laddie.

> On his head a bonnet blue,
> Bonnie laddie, Highland laddie,
> His royal heart was firm and true,
> Bonnie Highland laddie.

The melody to *Hielan' Laddie* was so catchy that it has also been used as a working tune (sea shanty), usually to aid long and slow manoeuvres such as hoisting sails or hauling up the anchor. It was popular on the Dundee whalers, then later used in the 1830s and 40s as a work song for stowing lumber and cotton in the south-eastern and Gulf ports of the United States, but it also turned up on the docks of Quebec.

Highland regiments raised in the eighteenth and early nineteenth centuries employed many unique symbols to differentiate themselves from other regiments and enlisted distinctive music to announce their arrival, but as a result of standardisation that came out of the Childers Reforms of 1881, all Highland regiments of the

British Army were required to use *Highland Laddie* as their regimental march.

By the Second World War pipers had been banned from the front line after the high numbers of casualties during the Great War. Pipers had been slaughtered in their droves in the First World War and of the two and a half thousand pipers that joined up over one thousand pipers fell (with approximately five hundred killed and six hundred wounded). It's likely that the enemy figured out how much of a morale boost it gave the Scots – although impossible to quantify, some have estimated that a good piper was worth five hundred extra men!

These great losses to the piping community led the war office to restrict their presence on the front line in the Second World War. However, on D-Day on 6th June 1944, Lord Lovat was keen to hold up the tradition of having a piper at his side when going into battle.

On the Normandy beaches, Bill Millin was the piper attached to Lord Lovat (Simon Fraser) who was Brigadier of the Queen's Own Cameron Highlanders, No. 4 Commando. Lovat's father had raised the Lovat Scouts and had been President of the Piobaireachd Society during the 1920s, and so it's with this heritage, as the 15th Lord Lovat, that he ordered Millin to strike up on that day at Sword beach - and in so doing defied the War Office's orders! When Piper Millin queried his superior, citing the regulations, Lord Lovat is known to have replied that they didn't apply to them as they were both Scottish.

As shells exploded overhead and German snipers took aim, Piper Millin prepared for the landing. Millin remembered that when the ramps on the boat went down Lord Lovat ordered him to play *Highland Laddie*.

The Normandy Landings

The beaches were invaded by hundreds of thousands of young men, traipsing through the red stained sea, being picked off by the well-prepared and well-armed enemy before they even reached the beach. Mere seconds after stepping into the water the solider next to him was shot and was killed instantly. Millin was always amazed that he was never shot - not only did he march up and down the beach standing tall, but the sound of the bagpipes could be heard over the noise of the gunfire and he was the only solider wearing the kilt - the one his father had worn while fighting in the First World War. After *Highland Laddie*, Piper Bill played *The Road to the Isles* and *All The Blue Bonnets Are Over The Border*. Two captured German snipers later told the private that they did not shoot him because they thought he had gone mad and they had taken pity on him. From that day on Millin was affectionately called Mad Bill Millin.

Although Bill Millin was born in Canada in 1922, his Scottish family returned to Scotland when he was age three and he was brought up in the Sandyhills area of Glasgow, and later Fort William. He played the pipes at Shimi Lovat's (Simon Fraser's) funeral in Beauly in 1995 and Millin himself died in 2010 aged eighty-eight. His D-Day pipes are now displayed at Dawlish Museum, in Devon. Piper Bill presented his pipes to the museum along with his kilt, commando beret and dirk, and these items are still on display at the museum library.

Today *Heilan' Laddie* has become a form of welcome tune, often played on special occasions; for example - to greet a VIP at a highland games or to accompany the groom processional up the church aisle at a wedding. It can be played at different lengths, from the first part only as a short salute, to two or four parts in length and is often played at quick march time.

The 10th Battalion Highland Light Infantry Crossing the Rhine

This tune is a stirring and lively 6/8 march. Time signatures such as 6/8s are in compound time where the top number is divisible by three and the value of each beat is that of a dotted note. There are six equal parts in the bar, each to the value of a quaver or an eighth note.

The composition was penned by Pipe Major Donald Shaw Ramsay (1919-98) and Corporal J. Moore. At the start of the Second World War, Ramsay famously became the youngest pipe major in the British Army at the age of twenty after passing the course at Edinburgh Castle under the tuition of Willie Ross.

This pipe tune was written to commemorate the symbolically important event in the Second World War when British forces crossed the Rhine, the largest German river.

The 10th Battalion of the Highland Light Infantry (HLI) landed in Normandy as part of the 15th Scottish Division. They took part in Operation Epsom, engaging in heavy combat around Cheux, Caen and Falaise, advancing while fighting alongside the Churchill tanks of the 6th Guards Tank Brigade.

The tune was composed for the action that began at 02:00 hours on 24th March 1945. The 10th Battalion HLI crossed the River Rhine in Buffalo amphibian vehicles at Xanten and then advanced on to the Elbe River, making one final assault to cross the Elbe a few days before the surrender of German forces in northern Germany. The tune has become associated with victory in Europe and the end of the Second World War.

My grandfather, William (Willie) Gordon, took part in the Second World War and was in the 1st Battalion (The Glasgow Highlanders), Highland Light Infantry. He first served in France as part of the 2nd British Expeditionary Force (BEF) but was evacuated from Cherbourg on 18th June 1940. He remained in Britain and trained with the Mountain Division (52nd Lowland Division) until October 1944, when he took part in the capture of the Dutch island of Walcheren, and then South Beveland, which fell in November 1944. He went on to serve throughout the remainder of the North-West Europe campaign, crossing the Rhine and then taking part in the capture of Bremen in April 1945. He eventually returned to Glasgow on 16th January 1946.

H.L.I. Cap Badge

Like many of the original Scots regiments, the HLI has had a long and honourable history. The regiment can trace their origins back to 1777, when the 73rd, or MacLeod's Highlanders, were raised by John MacKenzie (Lord MacLeod) in response to the need for troops to fight in the American revolution but it was renumbered the 71st in 1786.

War in India led to the formation of the 74th Highlanders in 1778 and a set of bagpipes, believed to have been played at the mustering of the regiment by one Piper MacCorquodale, are in the collection of the National Museums of Scotland. For distinguished action at the Battle of Assaye in 1803, the 74th were awarded the Assaye Colour and they remain the only infantry unit to carry a third colour. The unit was re-formed in 1881, following the Childers Reforms, through the merger of the 71st and 74th Highland Regiments of Foot, which became its 1st and 2nd Battalions respectively.

In 1923, the regiment's title was expanded to the Highland Light Infantry (City of Glasgow Regiment) because it was drawing its recruits mainly from Glasgow and the western Scottish lowlands at that time. Even though the original regiments were highland units, since the new unit recruited in Glasgow it was given the lowland uniform of MacKenzie tartan trews, not kilts. In doing so it became the only highland named regiment not to wear the kilt, a decision not reversed until 1947. The Glasgow Highlanders were an exception to the wearing of trews as they wore kilts during their early status as a territorial battalion within the HLI.

After the 1957 Defence White Paper, the HLI were joined with the Royal Scots Fusiliers in 1959 to become The Royal Highland Fusiliers (Princess Margaret's Own Glasgow and Ayrshire Regiment). The Royal Highland Fusiliers are now the 2nd Battalion of the Royal Regiment of Scotland (2 SCOTS) since March 2006. The Charles Rennie Mackintosh designed regimental museum is located near Charing Cross at 518 Sauchiehall Street in Glasgow.

Although *The 10th Battalion HLI Crossing the Rhine* is a foot tapping and spirited march, this tune is not as widely known as other marches, outside of the piping world, resulting in it having no lyrics, to the best of my knowledge.

Scotland the Brave

Scotland the Brave (in Gaelic *Alba an Àigh*) is a stirring 4/4 march. It allows the beginner-level player to practise the Taorluath finger movement on low A. The Taorluath is a strong embellishment that provides depth and is used to punctuate many tunes. The melody musters emotions of patriotism and is one of the main contenders to be considered as a national anthem of Scotland, having previously held that accolade for many years.

The tune was probably a flute solo originally and it is always listed as traditional in origin with no known composer. It was first published around 1911 in a Boys' Brigade pipe tune book. However, under a different title, *Scotland for Ever*, the tune appears to date from about 1891-5, when it was published in Norman Macdonald's Gesto Collection of Highland Music, although the saying *Scotland for Ever* dates back to at least the 1820s.

The words to *Scotland the Brave* were written in 1951 by the well-known Scottish journalist and broadcaster Cliff Hanley for the tenor singer Robert Wilson. Wilson needed a song to close his performance at a Scottish Christmas musical review at Glasgow's Empire Theatre. The lyrics make specific reference to the pipes in the second line which says Hear! Hear! the pipes are calling.

The song soon became popular with Scots people and was quickly adopted as an unofficial national anthem around 1955 and was still widely in use as the anthem until the turn of the century. *Scotland the Brave* was still being used to represent Scotland in the Commonwealth Games up to 2010. Prior to 1958 *Scots Wha Hae* was used and from 2010 *Flower of Scotland* has been used as the national anthem.

Scotland the Brave was played by a bagpiper during the opening of Peter Weir's movie Dead Poets Society (1989) as the pupils enter assembly. The tune is also the authorised pipe band march of The British Columbia Dragoons of the Canadian Forces. It is played for New York Police Department funerals and during the Pass-in-Review at Friday parades at The Citadel, which is a military college in South Carolina, USA.

Lion Rampant - the Royal Banner of Scotland

Following the reorganisation of the British Army in 2006, the tune was adopted as the regimental quick march of the Royal Regiment of Scotland, supplanting *Highland Laddie*. Presently, *Scotland the Brave* is a common tune to start 4/4 pipe band sets, frequently played alongside the scores *Flett from Flotta* and *Wings*.

Flower of Scotland

This haunting slow waltz was written in 1967 by Roy Williamson who was a member of a famous folk duo called The Corries, alongside Ronnie Brown. The 6/8 time ballad was released by The Corries as a single in 1974 and is written with reference to the victory of the Scots army, led by Robert the Bruce, over the King of England (Edward II) at the Battle of Bannockburn, just south of Stirling Castle, in 1314. In the lyrics Proud Edward's army is famously sent homeward tae think again.

There is a video of The Corries singing *Flower of Scotland* in 1969 from the lovely location of Ruthven Barracks in Badenoch that I recommend you watch. Roy Williamson (1936-90) plays the bouzouki and Ronnie Brown the bodhran. The bouzouki inspired The Corries to build the combolin, which is a guitar/sitar-like instrument of their own invention.

The song grew in popularity in the 1970s and 80s and supplanted *Scotland the Brave* when it was adopted as the pre-game anthem during the 1990 Five Nations Rugby Championship. The 1990 tournament culminated in a deciding match between Scotland and England, which Scotland won 13-7 to win the Grand Slam. It was officially adopted as the national anthem for rugby by the Scottish Rugby Board in 1993. What rugby fans started, football and other sports fans followed.

In June 2006 the Royal Scottish National Orchestra conducted an online poll on their website, asking visitors to choose a favourite song to be Scotland's national anthem.

With over 10,000 votes cast:

- *Flower of Scotland* came first with 41% of the votes
- *Scotland the Brave* with 29%
- *Highland Cathedral* with 16%
- *A Man's a Man for a' That* with 7%
- *Scots Wha Hae* with 6%

Other songs that have been suggested include *Auld Lang Syne* and *Freedom Come all Ye*. In more recent years, Dougie MacLean's ballad *Caledonia* has been gaining in popularity and some suggest this song, about homesickness – an emotion that Scots can feel acutely - should now be included as a candidate for the national anthem.

In 2004 lawyers acting on behalf of the devolved Scottish Parliament advised that it was within their legal competence to choose a national anthem, but in 2015 the Scottish Government stated that there is currently no official national anthem for Scotland. No doubt the debate will rage on.....

Highland Cathedral

Although this song has the sound and lilt of an old lament it is actually a very modern tune, having been written in 1982 for a highland games held in Germany. This very popular melody is in 4/4 time signature and was composed by Uli Roever and Michael Korb, two German musicians from Berlin. Korb always had a special liking for bagpipe music, and when he finished school in 1974 and went to Berlin, he immediately took lessons with the pipe major of a Scottish battalion based in Germany.

Since the composers' original release in 1982, the tune has been recorded more than eight hundred and fifty times. The Royal Highland Fusiliers were based in Berlin, and its military band, with Pipe Major Gavin Stoddart, were the first regiment to cover *Highland Cathedral* on their album Proud Heritage, released in 1986.

The first set of lyrics to *Highland Cathedral* were written by the tenor singer and composer Ben Kelly of Inverness in 1990. Although there are now a few different versions of lyrics available, Ben Kelly's lyrics describe the moment in history, namely the Union of the Crowns in 1603, when James VI of Scotland also became James I of England and Ireland. In this fictional reconstruction, all clan chiefs were asked to meet the King secretly at the St. Columba Church in Glasgow. There, they pledged to live in peace and end their constant feuding. This peace unfortunately lasted only as long as the King's reign. Due to the size, grandeur and its association with Gaeldom and the Gaelic language, St Columba's Church on St Vincent Street in Glasgow is popularly known as the Highland Cathedral.

Highland Cathedral was chosen as the Royal Hong Kong Police Anthem under British rule, which ended in 1997. It was played at a ceremonial lowering of the governor's flag at Chris Patten's official residence, Government House, on the last day of British rule.

It has become a very common choice to be played at weddings and, notably, the pop star Madonna chose *Highland Cathedral* for her wedding ceremony. Madonna was married at Dornoch Cathedral in December 2000 where she was entertained by Callum Fraser (aka Spud the Piper). *Highland Cathedral* also featured in the 1994 British film production Four Weddings and a Funeral.

The melody is now so well liked that it has been proposed, by some, as a new Scottish national anthem to replace the previous unofficial anthems of *Scotland the Brave* and *Flower of Scotland*. Whether or not it is adopted as the national anthem, the tune is here to stay as a popular favourite in the Royal Edinburgh Military Tattoo, where it has featured commonly since 2004.

The Crags of Tumbledown Mountain

This 4/4 march is a relatively modern composition, having been written by Pipe Major James Riddell in 1982. He composed this tune on the back of a cigarette packet at the Battle of Mount Tumbledown in the Falkland Islands. In penning this fine composition, Riddell followed a long tradition in which pipe majors were encouraged to write tunes to commemorate any actions in which their regiments had been engaged.

On 1st May 1982, the biggest naval action to take place since the Second World War began in the South Atlantic. Mount Tumbledown was the site of the largest battle of the Falklands War and it was one of a series of engagements that took place during the British advance towards Port Stanley. The battle lasted eight hours, after the British got pinned down, and only drew to a close after the Scots Guards mounted a swift and ferocious assault of the hilltop, scattering the Argentine 5th Marine Battalion before them.

By the end of the battle, the 2nd Battalion Scots Guards had eight dead and forty-three men wounded. The Welsh Guards had one dead, the Royal Engineers had also lost one, and the Gurkhas had sustained thirteen wounded. Twelve pipers were among the fighting troops that day on Tumbledown Mountain and after the fighting was over, James Riddell walked to the top of Mount Tumbledown to commemorate the battle and in doing so christened his new tune.

Argentina eventually surrendered to the United Kingdom on 12th June 1982. By the end of the war 258 British troops were killed and 777 wounded. Argentina lost 649 soldiers, 1068 were wounded and 11,313 captured.

James Riddell (1946-97) was the Pipe Major of the 2nd Battalion Scots Guards and is buried in his hometown of Stonehaven, in the north-east of Scotland.

O Tumbledown was tall and a strong defence did stand,
But Tumbledown did fall to brave Scots Guardsmen,
O Tumbledown was tall, the Argentines had played their hand,
But the crags and rocks, they were no Stonehaven.

At sea for a month, the Atlantic she did roar,
Britain had thought that wars were over,
But winter had come, leaving summer on the shore,
At the crags and rocks, of beautiful Stonehaven.

Crag to crag, rock to rock, through the wind and snow,
Crag to crag, trying to free Port Stanley,
Crag to crag, rock to rock, forward they did go,
But the crags and rocks, they were no Stonehaven.

O Tumbledown was tall and a strong defence did stand,
But Tumbledown did fall to brave Scots Guardsmen,
O Tumbledown was tall, the Argentines had played their hand,
But the crags and rocks, they were no Stonehaven.

The Palace of Falkland is such a bonnie sight,
A reminder of islands so distant,
But fae palace tae war, and noo the sodjer's plight,
In the crags and rocks, there was no Stonehaven.

Crag to crag, rock to rock, advancing through the night,
Crag to crag, trying to free Port Stanley,
Crag to crag, rock to rock, the gallant guards did fight,
But the crags and rocks, they were no Stonehaven.

O Tumbledown was tall and a strong defence did stand,
But Tumbledown did fall to brave Scots Guardsmen,
O Tumbledown was tall, the Argentines had played their hand,
But the crags and rocks, they were no Stonehaven.

The soldier's but a pawn, high heid yins play the chess,
Moving a' the pieces from safe distance,
But their moves wid be mair canny if they had to stand and fight!
In the crags and rocks, they widnae have their havens.

Crag to crag, rock to rock, their flares lit up the night,
Crag to crag, trying to free Port Stanley,
Crag to crag, rock to rock, wi' bayonets shining bright,
But the crags and rocks, they were no Stonehaven.

I have written these words to *The Crags of Tumbledown Mountain* as a tribute to the late James Riddell and his fellow men. It is a token of thanks for the bravery and sense of duty these men demonstrated during the Falklands War.

The composition is rare in that it is a 4/4 march with three parts. This brings a unique quality to the overall structure of the tune and has led me to write nine stanzas in sets of three in my best effort to complement Jimmy Riddell's fine work.

It has become popular to play this 4/4 at quick march tempo (especially at tattoos), but in order to sing all the words and syllables written above I suggest a slightly slower pace, moderated to around 90 beats per minute or so.

Acknowledgments

I am very grateful to those I have learned from and played pipes with over the years, and in particular want to make mention of the late Dr John Lawson, Pipe Major of Rubislaw Pipe Band, who greatly encouraged me to write this book. John gave huge amounts of his time and energy to promote and sustain piping and pipe bands in the north-east of Scotland.

The members of the Copenhagen Caledonian Pipe Band are thanked kindly for a warm and friendly welcome to Denmark (and in particular Niels Braunstein for multiple lifts to and from piping practice and engagements!)

Thanks go to Sam Cooper, friend and fellow geologist/piper, who assisted me by drawing the musical notation used in the book and also to Campbell Parker of Ballater for taking the front cover photograph.

Sincere thanks go to Bryn Wayte of Deeside Books for agreeing to help me publish my first book and for being such a patient and diligent editor.

Lochaber Axe

About the Author

Stuart Gordon Archer was born in Glasgow in 1972, and later attended Kingussie High School in the Scottish Highlands.

In 1994, he obtained a first class Honours in Geology and Geography from the University of Glasgow. An MSc and PhD were later gained from the University of Aberdeen. Professionally, he has been engaged in the oil industry, working in Aberdeen, Houston and Copenhagen as an exploration geologist.

The author was taught the chanter by John Stewart of Aberdeen and has been active in the pipe band world for the past twenty years, having played for Rubislaw Pipe Band and Banchory and District Pipe Band. While working and living abroad he played with Bayou City Pipes and Drums in Houston, Texas, and the Copenhagen Caledonia Pipe Band in Denmark.

Stuart is based in Dinnet in Aberdeenshire, where he lives with his wife Alex, and daughter, Ellen. He now plays his pipes with Ballater and District Pipe Band.

stuart.archer@outlook.com

Basket-hilted Broadsword

A Timeline to Assist the Reader

(date can relate to when the tune was written or when the associated story happened)

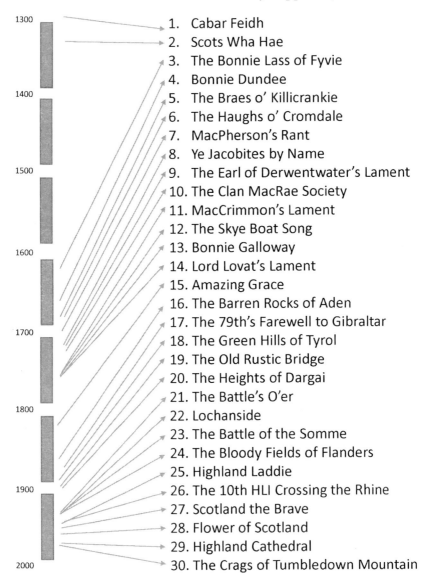

1. Cabar Feidh
2. Scots Wha Hae
3. The Bonnie Lass of Fyvie
4. Bonnie Dundee
5. The Braes o' Killicrankie
6. The Haughs o' Cromdale
7. MacPherson's Rant
8. Ye Jacobites by Name
9. The Earl of Derwentwater's Lament
10. The Clan MacRae Society
11. MacCrimmon's Lament
12. The Skye Boat Song
13. Bonnie Galloway
14. Lord Lovat's Lament
15. Amazing Grace
16. The Barren Rocks of Aden
17. The 79th's Farewell to Gibraltar
18. The Green Hills of Tyrol
19. The Old Rustic Bridge
20. The Heights of Dargai
21. The Battle's O'er
22. Lochanside
23. The Battle of the Somme
24. The Bloody Fields of Flanders
25. Highland Laddie
26. The 10th HLI Crossing the Rhine
27. Scotland the Brave
28. Flower of Scotland
29. Highland Cathedral
30. The Crags of Tumbledown Mountain